.50
KD

enjoying TRACK AND FIELD SPORTS

enjoying TRACK AND FIELD SPORTS

by the Diagram Group

PADDINGTON PRESS LTD

NEW YORK & LONDON

Library of Congress Cataloging in Publication Data

Diagram Group.
  Enjoying track and field sports.

  Includes indexes.
  SUMMARY: An illustrated guide to track and field
events for participants and spectators. Describes the
events and covers such topics as skills, techniques,
tactics, training, and clothing.
  1. Track—Athletics.   [1. Track and field]
I. Title.
GV1060.5.D52   1979   796.4'2   79–10371

ISBN 0 448 22207 8 (U.S. and Canada only)
ISBN 0 7092 0152 4

Printed and bound in the United States.

In the United States
PADDINGTON PRESS
Distributed by
GROSSET & DUNLAP

In the United Kingdom
PADDINGTON PRESS

In Canada
Distributed by
RANDOM HOUSE OF CANADA LTD.

In Southern Africa
Distributed by
ERNEST STANTON (PUBLISHERS) (PTY.) LTD.

In Australia and New Zealand
Distributed by
A.H. & A.W. REED

Foreword

The starting gun cracks through the stadium and ten bodies sprint forward, stretching with every ounce of energy as they clear the first hurdle. In the center of the track a high jumper lopes into his approach, gathers momentum, springs and arches backward over the crossbar. The crowd gasps as he narrowly misses it with his heel, but he's over! Up goes the bar for the next round. Speed, strength, stamina and agility are at the heart of every track and field event—whether in the sleek fluid grace of pole vaulting or sprinting, or the action-packed leap of the long jump. Athletes may no longer train by bending iron rods or taming wild bulls, but they do share the same dedication to conditioning and the same desire to excel as their first Olympic counterparts. Indeed, one of the deepest satisfactions of track and field is in the preparation itself—the joy of feeling yourself grow fitter, faster and stronger with each training session. And once you're ready, there are few things that compare with the thrill of competition.

This book presents the world of track and field sports in its entirety, providing young athletes with a complete step-by-step breakdown of the skills, techniques, training procedures and rules of competition for each event. In addition to the two main sections on track and field, there are also sections on athletics for the disabled and handicapped, for youngsters, and for those without easy access to athletics facilities.

We would like to thank those people in the world of track and field who have acted as our consultants. We hope that we have conveyed their advice as well as their wish to help everyone discover all the joys of track and field.

Editor	Ann Kramer
Copy Editor	Gail Besley
Picture Researcher	Enid Moore
Indexer	Mary Ling
Designers	Alan Cheung, Pauline Davidson
Art Editor	Janos Marffy
Artists	Stephen Clark, Alan Harris, Brian Hewson, Richard Hummerstone, Susan Kinsey, Graham Rosewarne, Anne and Michael Robertson, Diana C. Taylor
Art Assistant	Ray Stevens
Picture Credits	Anglo-Chinese Educational Institute
	Barnaby's Picture Library
	British Sports Association for the Disabled
	Tony Duffy – Allsports
	Mansell Collection
	Radio Times Hulton Picture Library
	the Spastics Society (Maria Bartha)
Consultants	Jim Alford BA, former National Coach
	John Greatrex, South London Harriers
	Paul Holland and John Wild, Highgate Harriers

Contents

Introduction

History of athletics

Tests of speed and strength have always been popular; the Olympic Games are known to have existed in 776 BC, and these were only a formal organization of sports that men must have been enjoying for years. Medieval fairs included many feats of strength and endurance, although they were not always serious—shin-kicking and grinning contests were very popular!

In 1812 a military college at Sandhurst, England, began an annual sports day, and in 1817 the world's first athletics club was set up in Norfolk. Rugby school in England started a cross-country race, and several schools followed suit by introducing athletics into their curricula. Later in the century the sport of athletics spread to the United States and Canada, and by 1900 the sports rivalry among American colleges had produced standards that excelled the British.

In 1896 the first modern Olympic Games were celebrated in Athens; the aim of their founder, Baron Pierre de Coubertin, was to revive the ancient Olympic ideals, and the Games have developed into the premier international sports meeting.

Women began appearing in athletics around 1900, but public disapproval (and rather cumbersome fashions!) held back the development of their opportunities for several years. Nowadays the grace and suppleness of the women is as much admired as the speed and endurance of the men, and with the spread of junior and intermediate contests, athletics has truly become a sport that the whole family can take part in.

Formal athletics events are divided into two groups: track and field. The track events are those that require speed against other athletes, while in the field events the athletes compete one at a time in jumping and throwing trials. In addition to track and field events, this book covers cross-country running and orienteering, two "fringe" athletics activities.

running

Running events range from the 100m sprint (covered in about 45 strides), to the 26 miles and 385yd of the marathon, during which the runner's feet hit the ground nearly 30,000 times. Races up to and including the 400m are classified as sprints, and have their own special running technique.

hurdles

Olympic hurdling events are the 110m (100m for women), the 400m, and the 3000m steeplechase. The steeple-chase consists of a mixture of hurdles and water jumps; the hurdles for this event are more robust than for the others, and the runners can either step onto them or jump them.

walking

The race walks generally take place on roads rather than on the formal track. The main characteristic of walking style is that the runner's front foot must touch the ground before he lifts his rear foot. Olympic race walks are the 20km and the 50km.

jumping

There are two types of jumping events; those for height (high jump and pole vault) and those for distance (long jump and triple jump). Women compete only in the high jump and long jump.

throwing

The throwing events consist of javelin, discus, hammer and shot. Each event has its own very specialized technique and rules for throwing. Women take part in all the throwing events except the hammer.

decathlon and pentathlon

The decathlon is a two-day contest for men, and comprises 100m, long jump, shot, high jump, 400m, 110m hurdles, discus, pole vault, javelin and 1500m. The pentathlon is a contest for women, and consists of 100m hurdles, shot, high jump, long jump, and 800m.

cross-country running and orienteering

These are not Olympic events, but they are activities related to athletics in their requirements of speed, mobility and stamina. Both sports are rapidly becoming more and more international as requirements and rules are standardized.

There are various safety rules that should be observed when you are taking part in athletics, especially if you are practicing in spaces that are not specifically designed for athletics—e.g. an ordinary field or an indoor gymnasium. Many of the rules are common sense, but it is worth taking note of them all. As far as keeping yourself in condition goes, make sure that you eat a sensible diet, get plenty of sleep, and never over-exert yourself—especially when recovering from an illness or injury. Always warm your muscles up with a few general exercises before you begin training, and keep yourself and your clothes clean to avoid picking up or spreading any infections in the showers or changing rooms.

running

1 It is advisable not to run in bare feet, even though the rules allow you to. On grass or other outdoor tracks, you may step on sharp or dangerous objects, or get the spikes of someone else's running shoe through your foot; indoors, much running on hard surfaces in bare feet can lead to trouble with the arches and insteps.

2 Ensure that any hurdles you are using will fall easily forward—away from the runner—if he knocks them.

jumping

3 The bar used for high jump must always fall at the slightest touch from either side, to avoid injuring the jumper if he falls across it. Thick foam mattresses must be used for the Fosbury Flop and similar jumps, and for pole vault.

4 Learn how to land without jarring – bend the knees or roll if you land on your feet. Do not jump from a wet surface or with wet soles. Do not jump before people have moved away from the jump. Do not distract someone who is jumping or about to jump.

throwing

5 Always err on the side of caution in the throwing events; for instance, stand well clear of the javelin run-up as well as the throwing area itself. Do not move until the object has landed. Do not throw if anyone moves into the landing area, and do not throw in bare feet in case your grip slips; a dropped shot could easily break your foot.

6 In main competitions, a net is provided for the hammer and discus, because slips and breakages can occur. Always stand behind the line of throw even when a net is being used.

Track events

At competitive level, athletic sports are divided into track and field events. As their name suggests, the track events are nearly all performed on a standard marked-out track or circuit. The track events comprise sprints, relays, hurdles, steeplechase, and middle and long distance runs. Walking is also classed as a track event, but in practice normally takes place on roads rather than a track.

Speed is the common denominator in all the track events. As an athletics event, running has been performed since the earliest days; the ancient Greeks featured both short sprints and long strenuous runs in their Games. In some ways, running is the most natural of all the athletic sports; it utilizes basic body skills, and fulfils the human need to compete—either against one's own standards or against other people.

All the track events are outlined in the following pages, along with their international rules, techniques, and training requirements. If you can run, and enjoy running, one of the events may be suitable for you. But don't expect to break world records overnight; it takes time, training and enormous determination to become a champion. Instead, set yourself personal goals and work toward them; you will derive great satisfaction and enjoyment from achieving them.

Sprinting

Sprinting is defined as "running at top speed," but, as no-one can maintain peak speed for more than about 25 yards (22.86 meters), in practice sprinting means running a relatively short distance at as near peak speed as possible. The standard sprinting events are the 100m, 200m, and 400m. Anyone can run, but to run as fast as these events demand takes a surprising amount of skill and ability.

shoes
Spiked running shoes are generally worn, with a maximum of six spikes in the sole.

pistol
Races are started by a pistol, or similar apparatus, fired upward into the air.

clothing
Running shorts and a vest are generally worn. They must be clean and non-transparent.

starting blocks
Starting blocks can be used for races up to and including the 400m. They must be made of rigid materials; they can be adjustable, but must have no springs. Both the athlete's feet must touch the ground at the start.

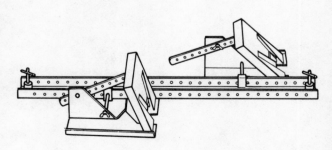

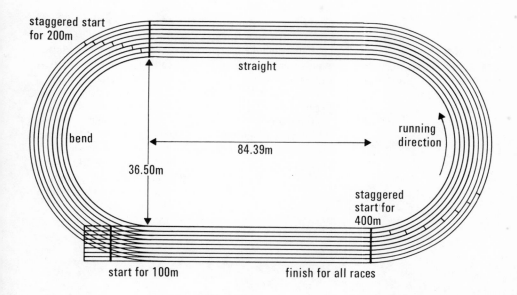

staggered start
for 200m

straight

bend

running
direction

84.39m

36.50m

staggered
start for
400m

start for 100m

finish for all races

track

The track shown here is a
standard 400m track with
straights of 84.39m and
curves of 36.50m diameter.
The track must be at least
7.32m wide, and the inner
edge should be clearly
marked with a border of
cement, wood or chalk,
depending on whether the
track is cinder or grass.
The track is measured 30cm
outward from the inner
border. The outer lanes are
measured 20cm from their
respective borders. The
lanes must not be less than
1.22m wide.
All races are run counter-
clockwise around the track.
The 100m is run on the
straight; the 200m is run
either on a straight track or
round a left-hand curve; the
400m is run on a circular
track round a left-hand
curve.

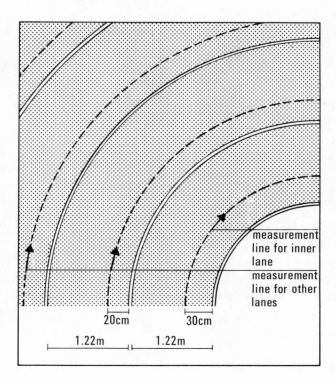

measurement
line for inner
lane

measurement
line for other
lanes

20cm

30cm

1.22m

1.22m

Sprinting rules

distances

These are measured from the edge of the starting line farthest from the finish to the edge of the finish line nearest the start.

heats

Preliminary rounds (heats) are held when there are too many competitors for a satisfactory single-round competition. Only in circumstances approved by the referee may a competitor take part in a heat other than that in which his name appears in the program.

start

Races run around bends have curved or staggered starts so that all competitors run the same distance. The starter, in his own language, gives the commands "on your marks" and "set" in all races up to and including the 400m; for longer races only "on your marks" is used. The pistol is fired when the competitors are all steady in position.

false starts

It is a false start if a competitor fails after a reasonable time to comply with the command "set," or starts before the pistol is fired. Competitors are recalled by a pistol shot after a false start. The competitor(s) responsible must be warned; a competitor is disqualified after causing two false starts.

lanes

All the individual races shorter than 800m are run completely in lanes. Lanes are decided by lot. Any competitor who deliberately leaves his lane is disqualified; if the offense was not deliberate, disqualification is at the referee's discretion.

check marks

These may be placed on or beside the track for relay races only.

leaving the track

Any competitor who voluntarily leaves the track or course may not then continue running in a race.

obstruction

A competitor who jostles, runs across, or otherwise obstructs another competitor is liable to disqualification. After a disqualification the referee may order the race to be rerun, or, in the case of a heat, permit any affected competitor to compete in the next round.

assistance

Intermediate times may be given only by an official timekeeper. Track competitors will be disqualified for receiving any other assistance from persons within the arena.

timing

Electrical timekeeping equipment is used for the Olympic Games and some other major meetings; otherwise timing is by timekeepers using stopwatches. Times are taken from the flash of the pistol to the instant when the athlete's torso is seen to reach the finish. Races up to and including the 400m are timed to 1/100 of a second.

the finish

Competitors are placed in the order in which any part of their torso (as distinct from their head, neck, arms, legs, hands or feet) reaches the vertical plane of the edge of the finish line nearest to the start.

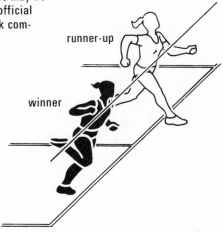

runner-up

winner

the start

On the whole good sprinters are born rather than made, but there are skills attached to sprinting which must be acquired and perfected. Mainly these are starting, picking up speed, and, in the 400m particularly, maintaining speed. Of these the start usually gets most attention; a slow start, particularly in the 100m, means a race lost. There are two ways of starting—a standing start and the crouch. The aim is the same in both: to get into full sprinting stride as fast as possible.

setting the blocks

Starting blocks are placed in the center of the lane, the front block about 12–18in (30–45cm) behind the starting line, the rear block about 16in (40cm) behind the front block. The front block is angled at about 50–60°, the rear block more steeply at about 80°.

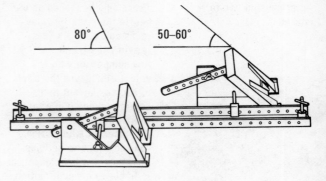

crouch start

a ''On your marks'': put your hands on the ground and crouch down. Place your feet on the blocks, stronger leg in front. Your hands must be behind the starting line, fingers turned out, thumbs turned in. Your arms should be straight, shoulder-width apart. Your rear knee should be on the ground, in line with the toes of your front foot, and both feet must touch the ground. Keep your weight over your hands.
b ''Set'': move your shoulders forward in front of your hands. Raise your hips higher than your shoulders. For an effective push your front leg should be bent at about 90°. Your hands should be as in ''on your marks.''

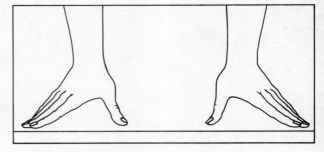

standing start

On the command "on your marks," place your stronger leg close to the starting line; place your rear leg about 12–18in (30–45cm) behind. Rest your hands on your knees. On "set," move your weight onto your toes; prepare your arms for running. At the gun, drive off.

starting on a curve

Technique is the same as for starting on the straight, but the positioning of the blocks is different. The starting blocks are placed at the outside of the lane, at a tangent to the starting line; in this way you can run straight for the first few strides. Of course, when starting on a curve the starting positions are staggered so that everyone runs the same distance. The 200m is usually run around one curve, and the 400m around two. For good curve running the technique is to keep as close to the inside of the lane as possible, (to minimize the distance), and to lean into the curve.

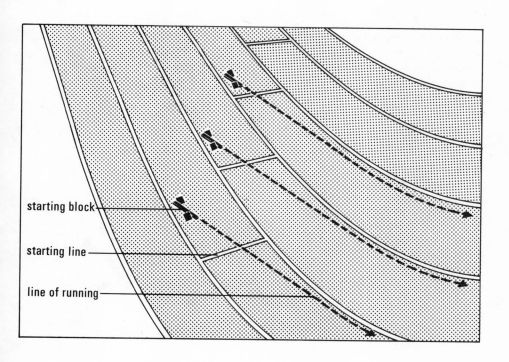

starting block

starting line

line of running

''on your marks''
Move into your blocks. Put
your hands on the ground
and position your feet. Place
your hands so that they are
behind the line, fingers in a
high bridge. Keep your
shoulders forward over your
hands, and your head in line
with your back.

''set''
Take a deep breath and hold
it. Move your shoulders
forward and raise your hips.
Brace your fingers, keeping
them bridged and behind the
line; fix your eyes on a
point about 15in (40cm) in
front of the line. Concentrate
on running rather than on
the gun.

fire
As the gun fires push hard
against the blocks and
pump your arms vigorously.
Pull the rear leg through to
take the first step; drive
hard against the block with
the front leg. Keep your
trunk low.

the finish
Concentrate on running
straight through the finishing
tape. The ''dip'' finish, in
which the trunk dips slightly
at the tape, is the most
common technique; used
properly it can win a race,
but avoid dipping too early
or slowing down.

to be avoided
Sprinting strides must be as
long as possible, but trying
to increase stride-length by
bounding (**a**) or reaching
out with your lower leg (**b**)
will tire you out and lose
you vital speed.

a   b

body action
Come out of the blocks running. Sprint with long, fast strides, keeping your knees high and your arms pumping forcefully from the shoulders, elbows bent at about 90°. Keep your trunk low for the first 8–10 strides, then move naturally into a more upright position. Your head should be relaxed in line with your shoulders.

100m
This needs as explosive a start as possible. Top speed can only be maintained for a short distance before dropping off slightly; once it does, use the driving action of your arms and legs to maintain as much speed as possible.

200m
This is best divided into three parts—an acceleration to top speed (about 60yd or 55m), a "coast" (about 100yd or 90m) and a flat-out finishing effort (about 40yd or 35m).

400m
This requires sustained sprinting and again is best paced, with a fast acceleration to top speed, a "coast," and a fast finish.

speed
Sprinting speed is achieved by the balance of cadence (leg speed) and stride length. Leg speed is innate, but stride length can be improved by increasing muscular strength and hip mobility.

driving practice
This is an excellent way of improving stride length. Use a standing start; lean forward and drive off. Keep your driving foot on the ground for as long as possible.

Relay

The relay events are normally the climax of any athletics meeting; the skill and precision of the baton changeover makes the relays exciting and unpredictable. One team of runners competes against another; a baton is carried, and passed from runner to runner. At international level the usual relays are the 4 × 100m and the 4 × 400m. The essentials of good relay racing are a fast, coordinated team, and accurate baton passing.

procedure
A team consists of four runners, each of whom runs one stage of the race. A baton is carried in the hand, and is transferred, in the takeover zone, from one runner to the next. If the baton is dropped, it must be picked up by the competitor who dropped it.
Composition of teams may be changed after a heat only in the case of injury or illness certified by the official medical officer. A team may change its running order. No competitor may run more than one stage in a race.

takeovers
The baton must be handed over within the marked zone. Runners about to take over must not start running more than 10m (11yd) before the take-over zone. After handing over the baton, competitors should remain in their lanes or zones until the course is clear.
Teams may be disqualified for causing an obstruction, or for pushing or giving any other assistance at takeover.

check marks
When a race is being run in lanes, a competitor may use a check mark on the track within his own lane, but nowhere else.
the start
At the start of the race the baton may be held over the line.

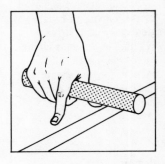

the baton
The baton is a smooth, hollow, rigid tube. It should not weigh less than 50g (1¾oz) and should not be longer than 30cm (1ft). It should be colored so that it can be easily seen.

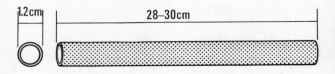

1.2cm   28–30cm

the track

The diagram below shows a 400m circular track, with the markings for the 4 × 100m and 4 × 400m relays. The 4 × 400m begins with a staggered start, and the takeover zones are situated at the same position on the track as the finish line.

The 4 x 100m is run entirely in lanes. 4 x 400m races are run in lanes as far as the exit from the first bend of the second lap.

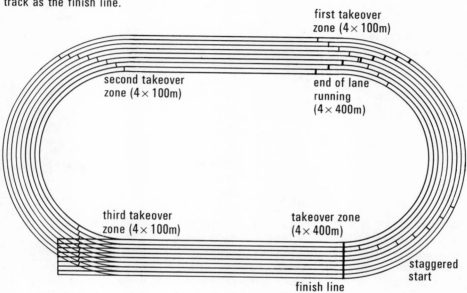

first takeover zone (4 × 100m)

second takeover zone (4 × 100m)

end of lane running (4 × 400m)

third takeover zone (4 × 100m)

takeover zone (4 × 400m)

staggered start

finish line

takeover zones (4 x 100m)

There are three marked takeover zones, each measuring 20m (22yd) in length. They are positioned at the 100, 200, and 300m marks. Before each takeover zone there is also marked an extra 10m (11yd) accelerating zone. The runner about to receive the baton may start running within this accelerating zone, but the actual exchange must take place within the takeover zone; if the baton is exchanged anywhere outside, disqualification results.

shuttle relay

No baton is exchanged in this relay; instead, takeover is made by a touch of hands. Contact must be made within a marked 1m (1yd) area at the end of each stage.
1 The waiting runner faces the incoming runner.
2 After takeover, the outgoing runner runs back along the course in the opposite direction.

baton passing

Fast, perfectly-controlled baton passing is the essence of relay racing.

The method most commonly used is the blind technique shown below; the receiver does not look at his receiving hand. The outgoing runner adopts the usual standing start, turning his shoulder to watch for the incoming runner.
1 As soon as the incoming runner reaches a pre-determined check mark the outgoing runner turns to the front and starts sprinting; from now on he will not look back.
2 The incoming runner shouts "hand," and the accelerating outgoing runner sweeps his hand back immediately, palm down.
3 The incoming runner thrusts the baton into the receiving hand.
4 The outgoing runner grasps the baton firmly, without slowing down.
5 The outgoing runner draws away.
6 The incoming runner eases up, and stays in his lane until the track is clear.

holding the baton

The first runner has to make a normal crouch start, while also gripping the baton. This presents the problem of how best to hold the baton while supporting body weight; the diagrams show four possible alternatives.

a High up in the hand, all fingers on the ground.
b In three fingers, thumb and forefinger on the ground.
c Between middle and fourth fingers—thumb, first and little fingers on the ground.
d In the middle finger—thumb, index, fourth and little fingers on the ground. The baton is held at one end, with most of its length sticking out of the front of the hand.

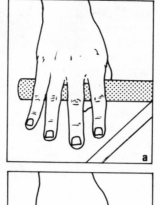
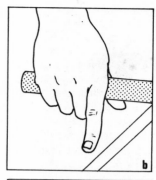
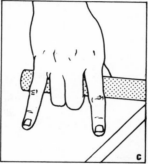
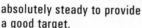
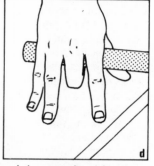

hints on baton passing

Points to remember are that the outgoing runner must start sprinting as soon as his approaching teammate hits the check mark, and that he must keep running steadily; the pass itself is entirely the responsibility of the incoming runner. Also, the outgoing runner must keep his receiving hand absolutely steady to provide a good target.

There is no need to change the baton from one hand to the other. Normally the first and third runners hold the baton in their right hands, and pass to the left hands of the second and fourth runners. Consequently, the first and third runners run on the inside of the lane, and the second and fourth runners on the outside.

check marks
For an effective blind baton exchange it is vital for the speed of the outgoing runner to blend with that of the incoming runner. To gauge the correct time to start the sprint, check marks are used. The position of the check mark is critical, but it is usually arrived at by trial and error. As a rough guide you can place a marker seven walking paces before the start of the acceleration zone. If you are the receiving runner, stand just inside this zone; as your partner sprints over the mark, turn and start running as fast as possible. When he calls "hand," sweep your hand back, fingers down, so that he can push the baton into it; the exchange should take place near the center of the takeover zone. You will probably have to adjust your check mark a few times before it is perfect. Outgoing runners usually adopt a modified crouch start (below). The supporting hand, which is placed on the line of running, is turned so that the four fingers are to the front, thumb to the rear. As the incoming runner approaches, the outgoing runner must face to the front and start running.

the exchange point
In order that the baton changes hands as quickly as possible, exchange should take place as the holder catches up with the outgoing runner. In general, good baton changes take place about 6–10ft (2–3m) past the center of the takeover zone.

As shown below, as soon as the incoming runner reaches the check mark the receiver starts running. At the center of the takeover zone, or at the call "hand," he sweeps his hand back; the exchange itself takes place about 6ft (2m) further on.

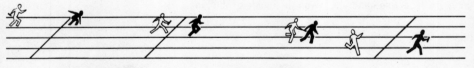

acceleration zone   takeover zone

the exchange

There are various ways of exchanging the baton; it can be pushed either up or down into the receiver's hand. But the most natural, and the safest, method is the "upsweep" used by most athletes today. The receiving arm is held well back, hand cocked slightly forward, fingers down. The baton is then swept up into the V made by the receiver's thumb and forefinger.

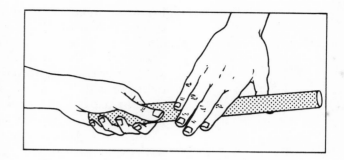

For a sprinter, the emphasis in training is on speed and endurance. Most of the training will consist of speed running, either on the track or elsewhere. Also, a weight training program and progressive resistance exercises should be incorporated to develop muscular strength. Certain aspects of technique – starting, bend running, and for a relay runner, baton exchange —must also be polished. Training alone does not make a sprinter; he must also develop confidence and the determination to win.

mobility
General muscular mobility helps to improve overall speed. During the off-season winter months, carefully planned mobility exercises such as sit-ups, leg cycling and trunk stretching should form part of the sprinter's training program.

strength training
Strength training should be carried out three days a week during the off-season. Weight training with dumbbells and barbells should be aimed at developing the upper body as well as the legs. Other ways of increasing strength include resistance running.

endurance
For a sprinter, endurance means the ability to maintain the maximum possible speed over a given distance. Because sprinting is an anaerobic event, with most of the race run in oxygen debt, the sprinter must get used to running as fast as possible when fatigued. The best way to improve this ability is by interval running—bursts of speed with short recovery times. This can be done on the track by repetition running and time trials, or in the country by a fartlek program.

improving speed

Sprinting is a mixture of leg speed and stride length. Essentially, speed is increased by improving technique and strength. But there are also running drills and speed activities such as running on a treadmill, running down a slope, and being towed, which help to encourage the muscles to move faster.

speed running

Speed running is aimed at improving overall speed. Basically it consists of repeated short, sharp bursts of flat-out running, with a period of full recovery in between. For example, after a 460 ft (140m) dash at full speed, an athlete needs 15 minutes to recover. This type of running tends to be done on the circuit, and is timed.

An example is shown below where an athlete runs as fast as possible for 15 seconds; the point reached is marked, and the athlete recovers. The exercise is repeated 5 times.

baton exchange practice

This is one technical aspect of relay running that must be perfected. The diagram below shows one method of baton practice. Four people stand in a line. The baton is passed down the line, moving alternately from right hand, to left, to right and finally to left hand. The four people should then turn around, then the baton is passed back. In this way, each person practices with each hand. The same exercise can be repeated with everyone jogging; there should be about 3ft (1m) between each person, and everyone should start jogging at the same time.

Hurdles

Basically, hurdling is sprinting over obstacles, the aim being to cross these barriers with as little break as possible in the natural sprint rhythm. This means that the hurdles are cleared with a step-over action rather than a jump; the movement should be absolutely fluid. Tall, long-legged athletes tend to make the best hurdlers, but the essential qualities are speed and suppleness, particularly of the hip joints.

rules

In general the rules for hurdling are much the same as for sprinting. Additionally in hurdling, disqualification occurs if a hurdler:
trails his foot or leg alongside any hurdle;
moves out of his own lane;
deliberately knocks down any hurdle with his hand or foot.
Where international hurdles are not used, a hurdler is disqualified after knocking down three hurdles; if international hurdles are used a competitor may knock any number, provided the rules are adhered to.

clothing and equipment

Clothing is the same as for sprinting—spiked running shoes of a standard design, shorts, and a vest. A track suit is also useful, particularly for winter training. In addition you should have your own starting blocks, and at least three hurdles to practice with. Special practice hurdles with hinged tops are available, but you can make your own.

track

The diagram shows a standard 400m track. All hurdling events are run in lanes. At Olympic level there are three events— the 100m, 110m and 400m. The 100m and 110m are run on the straight; the 400m is run on a curved track.

Each race involves clearing ten hurdles. In the men's 110m and 400m the hurdle heights are 106.7cm (3ft 6in) and 91.5cm (3ft) respectively; in the women's 100m the hurdle heights are 84cm (2ft 9in). There are also other standard races at junior and intermediate level.

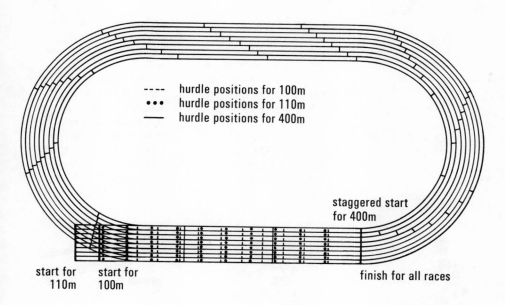

- - - - hurdle positions for 100m
• • • hurdle positions for 110m
——— hurdle positions for 400m

staggered start for 400m

start for 110m   start for 100m

finish for all races

hurdles

Hurdles are made of metal with a top bar of wood. They are designed so that a force of 3.6–4kg (8lb– 8lb 13oz) applied to the center of the top edge of the crossbar is required to overturn them. The height of the hurdle varies with the length of the race.

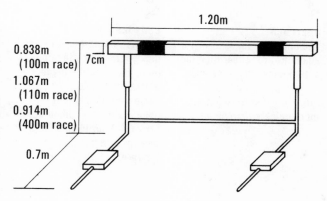

1.20m

0.838m (100m race)
7cm

1.067m (110m race)

0.914m (400m race)

0.7m

1   2   3   4   5

leading leg
The leading leg must be picked up high and fast for effective hurdle clearance. As you sprint toward the hurdle:
1 flex your leg at knee and ankle;
2 pick your leg up high and forward in the line of running; raise the other arm for balance;
3 bring your knee up to its highest point;
4 swing your foot forward, and
5 "throw" it at the hurdle. Choice of leading leg depends on personal preference, although it can be an advantage to lead with the left in the 400m. To keep your balance, lean into the hurdle at takeoff.

approach
The approach takes a certain amount of practice. Running action is exactly the same as for a sprint, but move into normal sprinting action more quickly than usual.

body lean
For faster clearance, as you pick your leading leg up high, you should dip your body at the hurdle. At the same time thrust your opposite arm and shoulder forward. Your head should be kept straight, facing forward.

clearance
The body lean should be maintained the whole time the body is in the air. As the leading leg moves forward, the trailing leg must be brought up and swung round laterally over the hurdle. As this leg crosses, the foot should be cocked at the ankle to avoid knocking the bar.

stride pattern
To maintain fluency and rhythm there must be a definite stride pattern. For the 100m and 110m, the stride pattern is 7 or 8 strides to the first hurdle, with 3 strides between hurdles. Your position on the blocks must match this pattern—if you are using 8 strides your leading leg should be on the rear starting block.
For the 400m the distance to the first hurdle is usually 21–24 strides, with 15 strides between hurdles.

follow-up stride
As the trailing leg crosses the bar, the rotary action should continue so that the trail knee comes through high and forward for a strong follow-up stride. The body lean should be maintained until clearance is completed.

1 **2** **3** **4**

100m and 110m (high hurdles)

This movement description is for a hurdler who leads with the left leg; adjust the instructions accordingly if you lead with the right.

1 Approach the first hurdle at full speed; keep your arms high.

2 Come up on your toes, dip your body forward, pick your leading leg up high and thrust your opposite arm and shoulder forward; push off from your right foot.

3 Drive your leading leg toward the hurdle, the sole of the foot aimed straight ahead; shoot your right arm out fully. Keep your body bent low; trail your right leg.

4 As your leading leg moves across the hurdle, start rotating your trailing leg from the hip.

5 As your lead foot begins to descend, pull your trailing leg over the hurdle.

6 Swing your knee round and over the hurdle; start straightening your body.

1 **2** **3**

400m

The hurdling technique for this event is essentially the same as above, but the athlete does not need to "dive" at the hurdles as strongly, so body lean is less pronounced.

1 Approach the hurdle with arms held high; lift your leading leg high and drive off with your right foot.

2 Stretch your arms forward; drive your leading leg forward and

3 cross the hurdle.

4 As your leading leg descends, sweep your trailing leg across the hurdle.

5 Keep your right leg folded, right arm down low.

6 As you land, pull your right leg through, knee high, arms ready for sprinting.

7 Drive off into the next stride.

7 Prepare to land, keeping
your arms low and your right
knee high.
8 Swing your right leg
forward, knee high.
9 Drive off hard with your
leading leg and reach out
with your right leg into the
next stride.

In this event, hurdling
technique and sprinting
speed are not as important
as endurance and pace
judgement. You also need
to find a satisfactory stride
pattern. This is more
flexible in the 400m and
will depend largely on your
natural stride length.
The approach to the first
hurdles is 45m (49yd) and is
usually covered in 21–24
strides; there are 35m
(38yd) between each hurdle,
and ideally this distance
should be covered in 15
strides, leading with the left
leg each time. But as
tiredness sets in, stride
length shortens and the
pattern may change to 17
strides.

Good hurdling technique is essential for this event; the aim of the steeplechaser should be to bring his steeplechasing time as near as possible to his flat racing time. This means getting over hurdles fast and efficiently. Today, at top class level, the time difference between the 3000m flat and the 3000m steeplechase is around 20–30 seconds. Generally speaking a young, rangy, fast middle distance runner, who hurdles well and enjoys cross-country running, will make a good steeplechaser.

courses

All steeplechase events are held on a standard 400m running track. The diagrams below show:
a the layout for the junior 1000m steeplechase, and
b the courses for the 1500m, 2000m, and 3000m steeplechases.
In the 1000m the track is lapped 2½ times and there

is a total of 8 hurdles and 2 water jumps.
The 3000m, for men, is the standard Olympic steeplechase event. It consists of 7½ laps, and there are 28 hurdles and 7 water jumps.
In the 2000m the course is lapped 5 times and there are 18 hurdles and 5 water jumps.
In the 1500m the track is

lapped 3¼ times making a total of 13 hurdles and 3 water jumps.
In each event there is a period of "free" running at the beginning of the race, during which no hurdles are crossed. The hurdles on that part of the track are put in position for subsequent laps once the runners have passed.

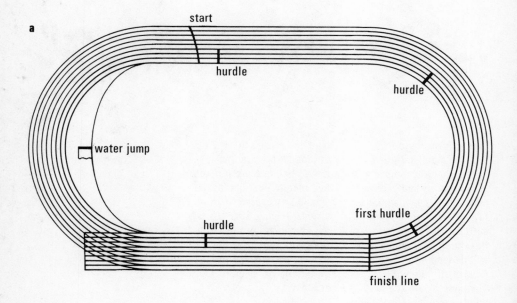

a

start

hurdle

hurdle

water jump

first hurdle

hurdle

finish line

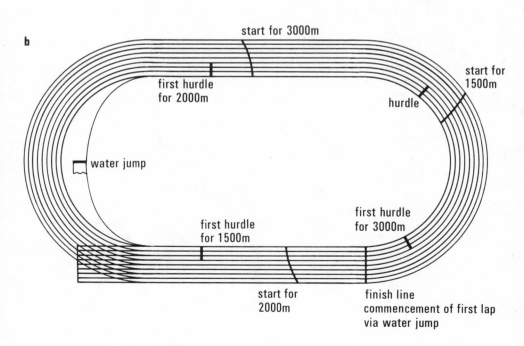

b

start for 3000m

first hurdle
for 2000m

start for
1500m

hurdle

water jump

first hurdle
for 1500m

first hurdle
for 3000m

start for
2000m

finish line
commencement of first lap
via water jump

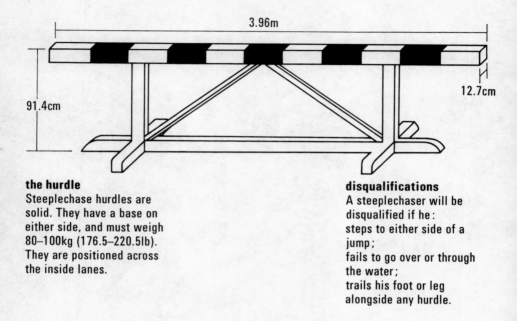

3.96m

91.4cm

12.7cm

the hurdle
Steeplechase hurdles are
solid. They have a base on
either side, and must weigh
80–100kg (176.5–220.5lb).
They are positioned across
the inside lanes.

disqualifications
A steeplechaser will be
disqualified if he:
steps to either side of a
jump;
fails to go over or through
the water;
trails his foot or leg
alongside any hurdle.

hurdle technique
The steeplechase is a tough
middle-distance running
event, and so hurdling skill
alone will not win it. The
hurdles are obstacles to be
crossed as efficiently and
quickly as possible.
Hurdling technique for the
steeplechase is similar to
that used for the 400m
hurdles (see p 40), but there
are some modifications.
Takeoff occurs earlier and,
because the hurdle is solid,
higher clearance is
necessary. Some athletes
get over the hurdle by
placing one foot on top and
stepping down; although
this is standard practice for
the water jump, it is not
advisable for hurdle
clearance.

the water jump
The water jump hurdle stands the same height as the other hurdles but is permanently fixed. Water jump clearance consists of putting one foot up onto the hurdle rail and driving off over the water so that only one foot lands in water, and dry land is reached in the first stride. The approach should speed up as the jump is neared. Takeoff must be accurate and you should use your takeoff (stronger) leg to land on the rail and push off again.

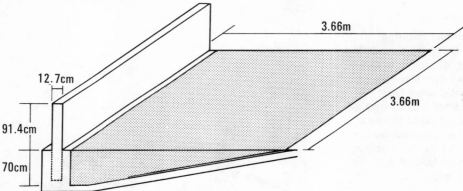

12.7cm

3.66m

3.66m

91.4cm

70cm

water jump technique
Takeoff should be 4–5ft (130–160cm) from the jump, but this varies with the speed of the approach. Use a check mark to locate an efficient run-up distance, during which you will prepare for the jump. Approach fast and rhythmically; lead with your stronger leg and land with the ball of the foot on the hurdle rail. You must wear spiked running shoes in order to get a good purchase on the rail. Keep your lead leg bent, pivot your body forward, and bring your trailing leg through. Push off with your stronger leg, and keep this foot against the hurdle for as long as possible. Reach out with the other leg and land in the water. Bring your strong leg through high, and sprint out of the water on the first stride.

Hurdling requires extreme muscular flexibility and mobility, particularly of the hips, groin, waist and shoulders. The exercises on these pages are specially designed for hurdlers, and should become part of a daily training routine. All these exercises should be performed using both the right and left leg so that both sides of the body are stretched and mobilized.

ground hurdling
1 Sit on the ground, thighs at right angles to each other, and each foot perpendicular to the lower leg.
2 Bend forward from the waist, pressing your chest down along the leading thigh. At the same time reach forward with your opposite arm.

trunk suppleness exercise
1 Start in the same position as above; keep your body relaxed.
2 Clasp your hands. Try to circle your right elbow around your right knee and foot. Then, without using your hands, lift your body with your leg muscles. Turn so that your left leg becomes the forward leg.

split
1 Adopt a split position, front foot at right angles to your leg, rear foot pointing forward. Look down. Balance yourself on your fingers.
2 Lean forward from the waist. Touch your lower leg, below the knee, with your chin.

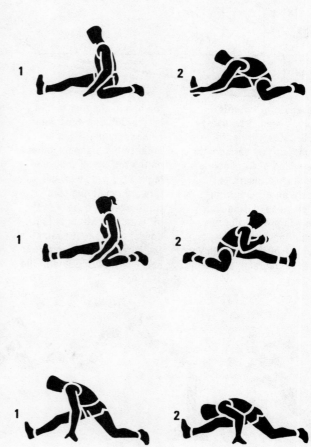

hurdle bends
1 Rest one leg along the hurdle rail; keep the foot turned outward.
2 Bend forward from the waist, and touch the ground with the hand nearest to the hurdle.

hip circling
1 Lean forward and grasp the hurdle rail.
2 Swing your trailing leg up.
3 Swing it round, performing one complete rotation; emphasize the thigh lift.

leg swinging
1 Grasp the hurdle rail with both hands. Swing your left leg across your body to the right; turn your right foot with the swing.
2 Swing your leg down and to the left. Turn your right foot with the swing.

leg swinging
1 Stand sideways to the rail and grasp it with your right hand. Swing your left leg loosely back from the hip.
2 Swing the leg forward. Keep your right leg straight, and your trunk upright.

lead leg

1 Stand sideways to the hurdle, your right hand on the end of the rail.
2 Lean forward and kick your lead leg up and over the hurdle. Lift your hand as your leg passes over.
3 Replace your hand as the leg descends, and straighten up.

trail leg

1 Stand at the end of the hurdle, left hand on the rail.
2 Bring your trail leg up, and lift your hand.
3 Rotate your trail leg over the hurdle; move your leg from the hip.
4 Bring your leg down and replace your hand.

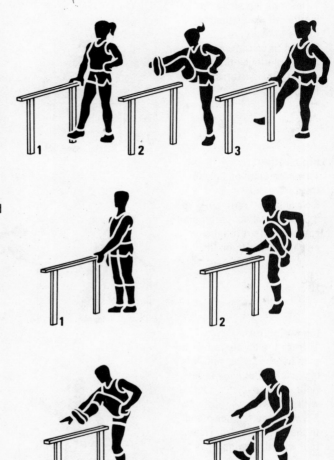

trunk flexing

1 Stand on the ground with the foot of your leading leg on the hurdle rail. Grasp the hurdle with your hands.
2 Lean forward; stretch your trunk and groin muscles.
3 As the hurdle tilts, hop forward. Then hop back.

hurdles training

Training for this event needs to be geared toward four main goals—speed, skill, suppleness and strength.

speed

Essentially hurdling is a sprinting event, and speed is vital. Training is much the same as for sprinting with the accent on short, explosive bursts of running, interval running, and fartlek. The faster the sprinter, the better the hurdler.

skill

Hurdling is an exact skill, and much of the training must be concerned with technique—approach, stride-pattern and hurdle clearance. Obviously, all technique practice must be done at speed.

suppleness

Good technique is impossible without muscular suppleness; all the exercises shown previously should form part of a training routine.

strength

Hurdling places considerable demands on the muscles, and the more force they can exert the better. Training should include working with weights, and all forms of resistance running. The exercise shown below, harness running, is an excellent form of resistance running, and also adds variety to training. While the athlete drives forward, the coach holds the harness and controls the amount of resistance.

steeplechase training

The steeplechase is a grueling event, and hurdling technique alone will not win it. It is a middle distance running event, and the hurdles and water jumps are obstacles that have to be crossed fast and efficiently.

A steeplechaser must be capable of fast sustained running for at least 10 minutes, and the emphasis in training must be on this ability. Tiredness is the steeplechaser's greatest enemy, and as well as speed running, training may include endurance running, fartlek, fell running, cross-country running and mountain climbs to build up the basic stamina required. The steeplechaser's first aim must be to achieve good speeds over middle distance runs (1500–5000m). Then he should aim to cover the comparable steeplechase distances in as near to his best times as possible. For this, technical competence in hurdling and water jump clearance is obviously essential, and specific technique practice must be incorporated into the training programme; ideally some technique training should take place when the athlete is tired. When hurdles and water jumps are used on a circuit for training, they should be placed as they would be in competition so that straight and curved approaches can be practiced.

The middle and long distance events hold an attraction for runners in a way that no other running events do. Perhaps it is because they provide a unique opportunity to prove oneself against all other runners, or perhaps it is because they are the most physically strenuous of the running events. To understand why they are so strenuous, it's worth knowing a little about the physiology of running. Normally the body is in a state of oxygen balance where the oxygen intake equals the oxygen consumed by the muscles. When increased work is done, the heart beats faster and pumps more blood to cope with the demand. But when an athlete runs at top speed, more oxygen is consumed than is supplied. Over a short distance this doesn't matter as the muscles can "borrow" oxygen (the oxygen debt) which is paid back after the runner breaks, gasping, through the tape. As the distance increases this type of running is no longer possible; the ability to win depends on the body's ability to deliver enough oxygen to the muscles. For the middle and long distance runner this means long, long hours of training, both to develop the circulatory system and to condition the mind and body to cope with fatigue.

Training for these events is long and hard; for the long distance runner in particular it can be a very lonely life as thousands of miles are covered in training. But despite this, or perhaps because of it, these events have produced a wealth of great runners. Among the middle distance champions some of the names that will always be remembered include Roger Bannister, whose 4-minute mile still holds an almost magical aura, Herb Elliott, Derek Ibbotson, Gordon Pirie, Vladimir Kuts and Jim Ryan; among the long distance champions are Ron Hill, Emil Zatopek and Jim Hogan, to name just three. For runners, it is these events that are the most exciting and the most challenging tests of skill, stamina, and courage.

events

The standard middle distance events are the 800 and 1500m for men and women, and the 5000m for men. The 10,000m is a men's event and falls halfway between middle and long distance. All these events are run on the standard 400m track; the diagrams show how many times the track is lapped for each event. With the exception of the first part of the 800m, none of the races is run in lanes.

equipment

Clothing and equipment are the same as for any of the running events. Spiked shoes are worn with a vest and shorts.

rules

The rules are quite simple; any competitor who jostles, obstructs, or runs across another competitor is disqualified.

starting

All these events have curved or staggered starts. No starting blocks are used for races above and including the 800m; instead a standing start is used, and the command is "on your marks," followed by the gun.

800m 2 times round track

1500m 3¾ times round track

5000m 12½ times round track

10,000m 25 times round track

running technique

Running style cannot be taught. On the whole it is personal to each individual and develops to suit his or her physical characteristics. But, style apart, there is a basic form that should be followed.

arm action

The action of the arms should balance that of the legs. The arms should be flexed at about 90°, and should swing backward and forward easily.

leg action

The movement of the legs should be relaxed, smooth, and economical. A good stride length must be maintained. The knees should point straight ahead and the athlete should make a ball-heel landing before driving off from the front part of the foot.

tactics

There are two basic ways of winning a race—to run in front for all or most of the race, or to come up from behind at the end. Which you use depends on personal preference, and experience. Front-running is not a tactic that suits everyone; it can be a very vulnerable position and it demands considerable confidence and determination. Because it is easier to follow someone else's pace, most runners prefer the second tactic.

the start

You should get into a good position as early as possible. The first 200m is usually run fast as each person jockeys for position; after this the pace settles for the middle part of the race. As a general rule, if you draw an outside position it is not worth trying to take the lead. Instead, work your way up through the other runners. At all times you should avoid being boxed in (1).

technique comparison

The diagram (left) shows a comparison between middle distance running technique (**a**) and long distance running technique (**b**). In the middle distance technique the recovery knee is lifted higher and the body lean is more pronounced; body lean tends to adjust itself naturally.

a   b

middle

During this part of the race it is generally best to run in third or second position. Often the best tactic is to run behind the leader's right shoulder (**2**); you can follow his pace, and from this position—if the circumstances are right—you can surge ahead and take the lead (**3**).

passing

If you do decide to pass, perhaps because the leaders are slowing down, you must do so as decisively as possible. You should accelerate rapidly from your position, and continue to accelerate for several meters. Avoid passing on a curve unless it is essential, since you will waste distance.

the finish

Your tactics at this point depend on your speed and condition. You should be ready to make your final burst any time after entering the back straight. You should aim for the element of surprise, and once you start to draw away you must not falter or slow down in any way.

Training for the middle and long distance events is more concerned with physical conditioning than it is with style. Methods of training include cross-country running, hill running, fartlek, long runs, interval running, speed/endurance running and speed, or repetition, running. Emphasis varies depending on the distance the athlete is training for; as a general rule, as distance increases the need for pure speed diminishes and the need for stamina increases.

training
The diagram shows a suggested ratio of anaerobic to aerobic training for four events. In anaerobic running the athlete runs almost entirely on oxygen "debt," and training for these events must increase his ability to do so. In aerobic running oxygen intake equals oxygen requirements,

and aerobic training therefore concentrates on improving oxygen-intake ability.

improving oxygen debt tolerance
Essentially anaerobic training consists of running at fast speeds with short recovery periods. In this way the athlete makes sure that his oxygen needs exceed the amount of oxygen taken in and that he, or she, gets used to running when completely fatigued. Some of the types of training normally used are outlined here.

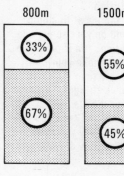
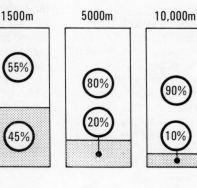
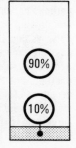

800m — 33% / 67%
1500m — 55% / 45%
5000m — 80% / 20%
10,000m — 90% / 10%

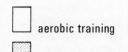

aerobic training

anaerobic training

Some training time must be devoted to improving basic speed, and this is best done by improving strength and muscular mobility, and by doing some technique practice. Weight training and resistance exercises improve strength, and mobility exercises make the muscles and joints more flexible, and help to produce an adequate stride length.

fartlek

This is a Swedish word meaning "speedplay," and one of its aims is to make training a little more enjoyable. It involves continuous running for a certain time rather than distance, at varying speeds through open country. The principle is the same as for interval running and the pace varies from fast sprints to easy jogs, at the discretion of the athlete. A beach or golf course is ideal for fartlek, and the course should contain a number of hills.

interval running

In this method the athlete runs fast, several times, over a set distance. Between each fast run is a recovery period of slow jogging. Distances vary from 100–400m, depending on the event being trained for, and the number of repetitions also varies. For an 800m runner a typical interval running session might consist of 6 x 200m at 28 seconds, with a 30-second jog between runs. The aim is to push the pulse rate up to 170–180 beats per minute during the fast run, and to let it drop back to 110–120 beats per minute during the jog. This helps to condition the heart so that oxygen-intake increases.

repetition running

This is much the same as interval running although the distances are usually longer and the repetitions fewer. It is a very intense form of training.

time-trials

These are a traditional form of training and can be flat-out efforts, or attempts to achieve a specific time target. They are normally run on the track.

improving oxygen-intake

Long, steady runs of 6–20 miles, once or twice a week, are the best way of developing the capillary system and improving oxygen-intake. They should be run at an even, steady pace of about 6–8 miles per hour.

The marathon originated in 490BC when Pheidippides made his epic, and fatal, run from Marathon to Athens with the news of the Greek victory over the Persians. As a modern athletics event it was introduced into the Olympics in 1896, and today it is the longest running event held at the Olympic Games. It is a grueling event requiring considerable stamina, endurance, and determination as well as careful and intensive training and preparation.

rules

The marathon is 42.195km (26 miles 385yd) long. The start and finish are usually in the arena, but the rest of the race is run on made-up roads. Distances, in kilometers and miles, are displayed to the competitors along the route. Competitors must leave the race if ordered to do so by the medical staff.

refreshments

Official refreshment stations are sited every 5km (3 miles). Fruit juices boosted with glucose are usually provided. There are also additional sponging points, supplying water only. Refreshments should be taken without stopping or interrupting the running rhythm, and the same applies to sponging.

technique

Despite its length, the marathon should be approached just like any other long distance run. Pace-judgement and concentration are essential. During the first few miles save your energy, find an economic running pace, and stick to it. At the same time concentrate on beating the other competitors rather than just staying on the course.

equipment

In 1960 the great Ethiopian runner Abebe Bikala ran the marathon barefoot in just over 2¼ hours. For most people this would be impossible and lightweight running shoes, cushioned at sole and heel, are essential. Vaseline can be used, on the toes or inside the shoes, to help prevent blisters. Shorts and a vest are also worn, a string vest in summer and a long-sleeved vest in winter.

pre-race diet

Most marathon runners now use a special pre-race diet to raise the glycogen in their muscles. Seven days before the event the athlete reduces his glycogen level with a long training run. For the next three days only fats and proteins are eaten. Four days before the event, the athlete switches to a carbohydrate-rich diet that will provide the necessary glycogen reserves for the last few miles of the race.

training

Preparation for the marathon means running thousands of miles a year. Training must include daily distance running of say 5–10 miles in the morning followed by a longer run of 15–30 miles at least three afternoons a week. The runner must also do a certain amount of repetition running, timed trials, and fartlek.

Despite its exaggerated appearance, competitive walking is basically the same as ordinary walking, but it is much faster. Whereas the ordinary person walks a mile in about 15 minutes, the competitive walker can do it in about 8 minutes, and can continue walking at this speed for a distance of 3000m.

shoes

Special walking shoes are needed with soles up to 13mm (½in) thick. The heels must not be more than 13mm (½in) thicker than the soles.

rules

Walking events may be held on a track or on the road. At international level there are two standard events— the 20km and 50km road walks.

The main rule is that walkers must maintain unbroken contact with the ground. Any walker whose action looks suspect will be given a caution.

disqualification

A competitor is entitled to one caution (signaled with a white flag), before being disqualified (signaled with a red flag).

Action is taken against a competitor after the independent recommendation of three judges, or two judges if one is the chief judge. In track races a disqualified competitor must immediately leave the track. In road races he must immediately remove his number. If immediate disqualification is impracticable, competitors may be disqualified immediately after a race ends.

refreshments

Approved refreshments may be taken at official refreshment stations in walking races over 20km (12 miles). Stations are sited every 5km (3 miles); no other refreshments are allowed. Additional sponging points, supplying water only, may be provided at points after 20km.

training
Training for walking consists mainly of distance walks, form walks, and speed walks.

distance walks
These are walks covering distances of between 5000m and 10,000m, and are aimed at improving the athlete's physical condition, especially his heart and legs.

form walks
These are aimed at developing good technique, and can take place over differing terrain as in fartlek. Ideally one technical point at a time should be worked on, with a slow-walk recovery period in between each stint.

speed walks
These are obviously designed to develop good walking speed which may be necessary during a race. During these speed walks, which should only cover 400–800m distances, good technique must be maintained.

action
The main point about race walking is that unbroken contact must be maintained with the ground. This means that the near foot must not leave the ground before the advancing foot has made contact.

As in the sequence below, the knee must straighten before the heel touches the ground. At each stride the hips should rotate fully, while the arms act to balance the body and are carried loosely. As the race speeds up the arms should be moved more vigorously. The body must remain upright, and the head absolutely steady. The walker should aim for an even, strong, steady pace.

Field events

Jumping events

Jumping competitions are among the oldest "athletics" events in the world. Jumping events are known to have existed in the ancient Olympic Games, and pieces of pottery have been found that illustrate athletes in classical Greece competing against one another in elementary long jump contests.

There are four jumping events—the high jump, pole vault, the long jump and the triple jump. Loosely they can be divided into two categories: vertical jumps, which are the high jump and pole vault, and horizontal jumps, which are the long jump and triple jump. Despite their differences in style and technique all four events demand the ability to combine speed and spring in order to achieve height or distance.

High jump

The high jump is a jump made over a crossbar suspended between two rigid uprights. There are five main jumping styles—Scissors, Eastern cut-off, Western roll, Straddle and Fosbury Flop. In competitive jumping the crossbar is raised after each round, competitors remaining in the event until eliminated by three consecutive failures.

judges
There are two or three judges, who make sure that the apparatus and landing area are in order and that all jumps are correctly made.

run-up
The length of the run-up is unlimited. Marks may be placed for run-up and take-off; a handkerchief, or similar marker, may be placed on the bar for sighting purposes.

procedure
Starting heights for each round are announced by the judges before the event begins.
Competitors may start jumping when they wish, and choose whether to attempt any subsequent height. Elimination occurs after three consecutive failures, regardless of the height at which they occur.

failures
A jump is counted a failure if the competitor (a) takes off from both feet; (b) touches the ground or landing area beyond the plane of the uprights without first clearing the bar (whether or not he makes a jump); (c) knocks the bar off the supports (even if he has landed before the bar falls).

measurements
These are made perpendicularly from the ground to the lowest part of the upper side of the bar. New heights are measured before jumping begins, and heights are remeasured after jumping if a record is to be established.

shoes

Comfortable non-slip foot-
wear should be worn;
jumping shoes with heel
spikes and plastic heel cups
are recommended for high
jumping. Using a heel pad
inside the shoe helps to
avoid bruising the heel.

crossbar supports

Crossbar supports must face
the opposite upright and be
flat or rectangular. The
crossbar itself may be
triangular in cross-section
or circular with square ends.
It should not weigh more
than 2.2kg (4lb 12·8oz)

layout

The layout of the high jump
area is shown below. The
measurements shown are
those recommended by the
International Amateur

Athletic Federation (IAAF).
The approach area (fan) is
usually an all-weather
surface. The landing area
must meet various safety
regulations and is generally
composed of foam cushions.
Any type of uprights may be
used but they must be
absolutely rigid. They should
extend 10cm (4in) above the
maximum height to which
the crossbar can be raised.
They may only be moved if
the takeoff or landing area
has been judged unsuitable.
The crossbar is usually
made of wood, metal or
fiberglass.

There should be a gap of at
least 1cm (¼in) between
the ends of the crossbar and
the uprights. If touched by a
competitor the crossbar
should fall easily to the
ground. It must always be
replaced with the same
surface facing upward.

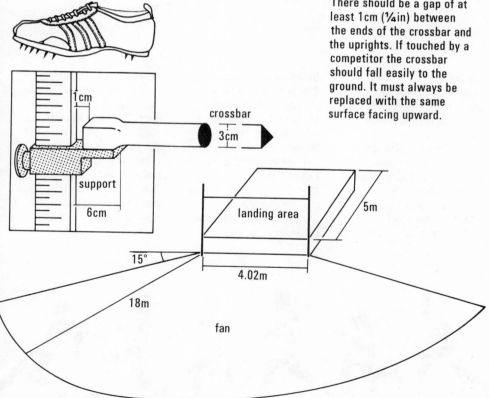

accuracy and direction

An accurate approach and takeoff is vital. To find your takeoff spot stand sideways to the bar; reach your arm out so that your fingers brush the bar. Run 5 strides at an angle of about 35–40° to the bar. Mark the fifth stride; run back and jump.

The direction of approach varies according to the jump. This approach (right) is for the Fosbury Flop and curves inward for the last 3 strides.

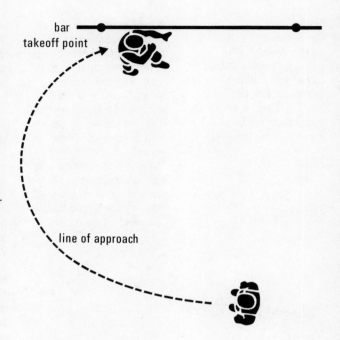

bar
takeoff point

line of approach

approach

The length of the approach run varies, although 7- and 9-stride approaches are the most commonly used. To start with, use a short approach run. During the first few strides the running style is not very important, although it should be fast and steady with no bounce or spring.

Straddle approach

The body should be leaning forward. It is the last 3 strides (shown below) that are the most vital. During these you do not accelerate, but aim to hold your speed and to "settle" yourself for takeoff. (It is advisable to place a check mark 3 strides from takeoff as a reminder to change running style.) These last 3 strides must be run flat-footed on the heels, knees bent. The body should lean back slightly, hips ahead of the shoulders; as a result, these strides are much longer than the earlier ones. Aim to take off so that you cross the bar at its lowest (central) point.

takeoff

Takeoff is the most important part of high jumping. Basically there are two styles:

a the force takeoff with a straight or bent leg used for the Straddle; and
b the speed takeoff with a bent leg used for the Flop.

a In the Straddle-style takeoff the takeoff foot is placed far ahead of the body. Leg, hip and trunk all lean back. As you arrive at takeoff the body straightens up and the arms and free leg add to takeoff by swinging upward. The free leg begins its swing from the hip, straightens at the knee and remains straight as it passes through the horizontal position.

b In the Fosbury-style takeoff the action is similar to that of the long jump. The takeoff foot is not as far ahead and the body remains vertical. The arms swing upward and the free leg drives up, but this time with the knee bent.

a

b

flight

There are five flight techniques—the Scissors, Eastern cut-off, Western roll, Straddle and Fosbury Flop. But essentially, once you are in the air there is nothing you can do to propel yourself further. The point of using any of these techniques is to raise your center of gravity as high as possible and to arrange your body in the most economic and efficient way so that you can clear the bar. The

Scissors technique is the least efficient and the compact Straddle and Flop are the most efficient.

Scissors

Most beginners start with
this technique; it is safe,
simple and natural.
Basically the bar is crossed
in a sitting position, the
takeoff leg being the one
farthest from the bar. But a
great deal of body weight
has to be lifted above the
bar to clear it which makes
it an inefficient way of
jumping. A point in its
favor is that it does not
need a specially-
constructed landing area.

Eastern cut-off

This technique is similar to
the Scissors; once again it
does not need a special
landing area. The outside
leg is used for takeoff, and
body weight is more evenly
distributed along the bar;
the jumper lands on his
takeoff foot. This technique
is rarely used today.

Western roll

This is a good jump
for relatively low heights.
Again it has the advantage
of a safe landing. In effect
it is a hop over the bar, the
takeoff foot being the one
nearest to the bar. It is a
compact technique, body,
head and arms going over
close to the bar.

Straddle
1 Leaning well back, rock onto toes of takeoff foot.
2,3 Bend takeoff leg, throw arms up, and swing free leg from the hips up and toward the bar.
4 Push off and leave the ground, turning the body to clear the bar.

5 Keep left arm, elbow bent, close to the body; bring left leg up.
6,7 Revolve the body over the bar, rotating head, shoulders and right arm toward the ground.

8,9 As right shoulder drops toward the landing area, straighten left leg to avoid dislodging the bar; roll away from the bar to land on side and back.

Fosbury Flop
1 Run in from the curved approach so that you lean away from the crossbar.
2 Bend free leg up and across.
3 Straighten takeoff leg.
4 As you drive off, turn the body with the back toward the bar, keeping your eyes on the crossbar.

5 Keep legs up and arms to the sides.
6 Drive hips up.
7 Clear the bar with head, shoulders, trunk and hips; keep legs bent at the knees.
8 Drop down toward the ground, straightening legs to avoid dislodging the bar.
9 Fall on back into the landing area.

The Straddle is the most popular high jumping technique and the most efficient; the straight-legged Straddle shown here is commonly used.

The technique tends to vary slightly according to the individual; an accepted alternative method is one in which the free leg is bent rather than straight at the takeoff.

Bringing the takeoff leg up and straightening it so that it does not dislodge the bar is the most critical part of the technique; it requires split-second timing and absolute coordination.

The Fosbury Flop—an entirely new style of jumping—was introduced into the 1968 Olympic Games by gold medalist Dick Fosbury. For this jump, a safe landing area—of foam rubber, not sand—is essential. Given this, the Flop is a surprisingly simple, natural and safe way of jumping. It is not a backward jump; in effect it is a back layout Scissors.

At take off the head should be parallel to the bar, and the body turns in the air. A fast approach run is essential; this is normally curved so that you arrive for takeoff leaning into the curve, rather like a cyclist going round a tight bend. The takeoff foot is well forward, ahead of the hips and shoulders.

Pole vault

It is said that East Anglian farmers were the first competitive pole vaulters, but this is uncertain. Modern pole vaulting dates from the 19th century; it was taken to the United States by Scotsmen, and in 1896 became part of the Olympics. Using a flexible pole, competitors vault over a crossbar which is raised after each round; it is a thrilling event that requires speed, stamina and good coordination.

equipment

Pole vaulting equipment has evolved a long way since the sport's birth. Early poles were made of ash or hickory fitted with iron prongs or tripods. These gave way to bamboo poles, and subsequently to the metal (**a**) and highly flexible fiberglass poles (**b**) used today. Most beginners start with a metal pole; these are cheaper, but have a limited vaulting height. Because of the two types of pole there are now two different vaulting techniques, although basic skills are similar. In competition a competitor may use any pole provided that it is smooth-surfaced; it may also be of any length or diameter. Typical dimensions are shown (**c**). The pole should be bound with adhesive tape to provide a handgrip but there should not be more than two layers of uniform thickness. Spiked shoes are recommended.

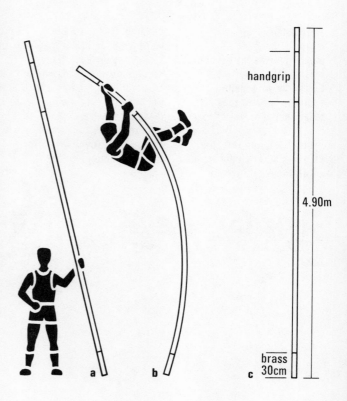

handgrip

4.90m

brass
30cm

a   b   c

run-up
The length of the run-up is unlimited. Check marks may only be placed alongside the runway.

judging
There are usually three judges; two adjust apparatus and record the vaults, the third watches the run-up and liaises with competitors.

procedure
Starting heights are announced by the judges before the event begins. Competitors may start when they like and can choose whether or not to attempt subsequent heights. Elimination occurs after three consecutive failures.

uprights
These must be rigid. They can be moved, but must never be more than 60cm (2ft) from the continuation of the inside edge of the top of the stopboard. The box is made of metal or wood, and is sunk level with the ground.

failures
A competitor fails if he: touches the ground beyond the box with his body or pole before takeoff; dislodges the bar during a vault; leaves the ground but fails to clear the bar; ''climbs'' up the pole as he leaves the ground.

crossbar
The crossbar must not exceed 2.5kg (5lb 8oz). If touched it should fall easily toward the landing area. Supports are smooth pegs with a uniform diameter not exceeding 13mm (½in).

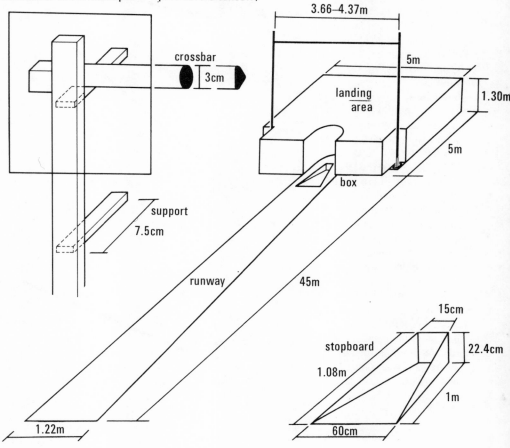

crossbar
3cm
support
7.5cm
runway
1.22m

3.66–4.37m
5m
landing area
1.30m
5m
box
45m

stopboard
15cm
22.4cm
1.08m
1m
60cm

carrying the pole

For the approach there are various ways of carrying the pole; four are shown here.

1 The low-point carry. This is probably the best for beginners, as the pole is easily maneuvered for takeoff.

2 The intermediate carry. This is the best way to carry the pole for a really fast approach.

3 The high-point carry. This allows good pole leverage and balance during the approach.

4 Cross-body carry. This method tends to slow down the end of the approach run as the pole has to be lined up with the runway before being "planted" in the vault box.

hand-hold

Finding the right hand-hold is a matter of experiment. With a right-handed person, the right hand is to the rear of the body, and the left hand in front. There should be a gap of about 2–3ft (60–90cm) between them.

The hand in front should be palm down so that the pole rests on the thumb. The pole should not be gripped too tightly. It is best to start with a low hand-hold, the right hand being about 8 or 9ft (2.5 or 3m) from the bottom of the pole. When running the pole should swing gently backward and forward.

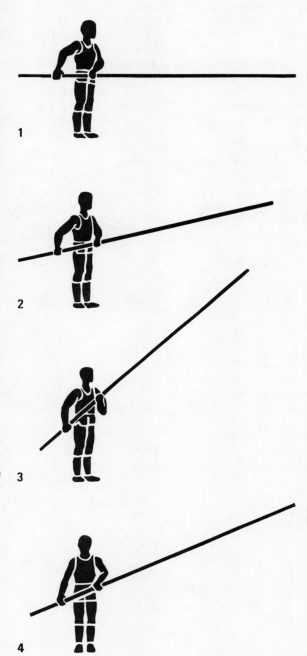

approach

Start by using a short 9-stride run-up. This gives an approach run of about 10ft (3m). The plan shown (1) is for a person who takes off from the left foot. Place the first check mark 3 strides from the starting point, and take off 6 strides from the check mark.

starting point   first check mark   takeoff

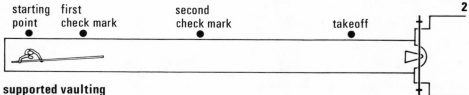

As you become more experienced you can lengthen the approach run. Plan (2) shows a 17-stride approach. There are two check marks: the first is 3 strides out from the starting mark, the second is 9 strides out. Takeoff is 8 strides from the second check mark.

starting point   first check mark   second check mark   takeoff

supported vaulting

Practice vaulting with a friend supporting the pole. As he holds the pole, make a short run onto the pole, hang, and swing up body and legs as you are swung vertically into the landing area.

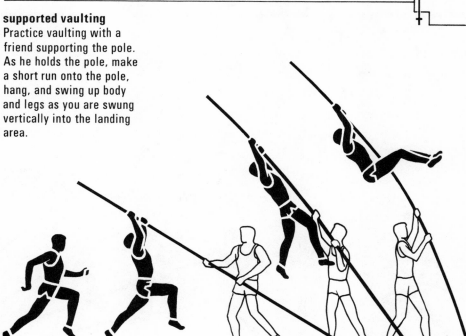

steel pole vault
1 Run up, keeping pole tip at approximately head height.
2 Start lowering pole ready for "plant."
3 Lower point of pole into vault box, pushing elbow of the bottom arm forward.

4 Thrust pole into box as left foot is coming to the ground; shift hands, sliding pole through left hand so that hands are close together. Bring right knee up and drive off from left foot.
5 Hang.
6 Swing up body and legs.
7 Keeping right hand higher than the left, pull on the arms, still swinging the body and legs.

8 Turn the whole body until the legs are higher than the head.
9 Push down and arch the body over the crossbar.
10 Keep body away from the bar, and release the pole.
11 Drop to the ground, throwing arms and head up and back.

If the takeoff foot is the left one, everything else takes place on the right; the pole is carried on the right side, the right hand is uppermost during the carry, and the vaulter swings to the righthand side of the pole after takeoff. With a right-foot takeoff, everything is reversed. The points to note are that the run-up should be as fast as possible; speed must not be lost as you prepare to plant. During the plant the hand grip should be quite firm, and the hands close to each other. Once airborne and as soon as the pole is almost vertical, you must tuck your legs up quickly, turn your body so that you are virtually doing a handstand on the pole, push hard, and arch your body well over the bar.

fiberglass pole vault
Adjust the instructions
accordingly if you prefer
your left hand at the
top of the pole.
1 Run up; move pole well
out in front, and as right
leg moves forward plant pole
overarm into vault box.
2 Keep right arm straight
during plant so that hands
are quite widely spaced.
Bend left knee and drive
off, swinging right leg
forward and upward.

3 Pull with right hand to
increase pole bend.
4 Swing legs upward,
keeping left arm slightly
bent.
5 Bend at hips and raise
feet above head.
6 Straighten both legs.
7 Pull up; flex arms at
elbows, driving body and
legs upward.
8 Rotate body toward pole.
9 Push body up.
10 Swing left leg upward
and right leg down in a
scissors action.

11 Complete rotation to
clear the bar; release pole.
12 Raise arms and shoulders
up and away from the bar,
and drop to the ground.

Although it is expensive, the fiberglass pole has revolutionized pole vaulting. Its main advantage is its "give" and flexibility, which make it almost like a catapult. Because of its flexibility a much higher hand hold can be used so that the user can leave the pole from a higher point. The main things to remember are that the pole must be well out in front before planting and that the hands are not to be shifted together; to avoid this, bind the pole with tape at the lower hand grip. When choosing a fiberglass pole it must be one that will bend easily, but not break. Poles are graded according to weight, and range from 85–190lb (38–86kg).

A safe landing area is vital for both aluminum and fiberglass vaulting; sand is fine for steel vaulting at low heights, but foam bags are essential for greater heights and for fiberglass vaulting.

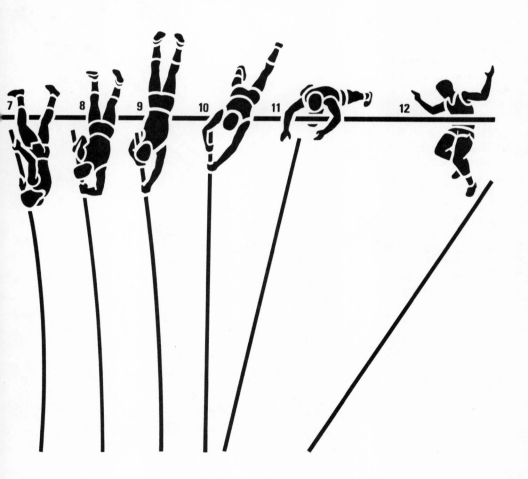

Long jump

The long jump is one of the oldest Olympic events, and technically it is one of the simplest of the jumping events. Essentially it consists of a very fast run, a spring, and a powerful jump; to be a successful long jumper you need a good sprinting speed and lots of springing power. In competitive long jumping each competitor has three to six attempts.

clothing

The best shoe is one similar to the ordinary sprinting shoe; use a sponge heel pad on the outside. For grass, heel spikes are essential.

landing area

The dimensions are shown right. The sand should be moistened before the jumping begins, and must be raked level with the takeoff board before every jump.

takeoff board

This is made of wood, to the dimensions shown in the diagram, and is sunk level with the runway. Beyond it is a tray of Plasticine or similar substance for recording foot faults.

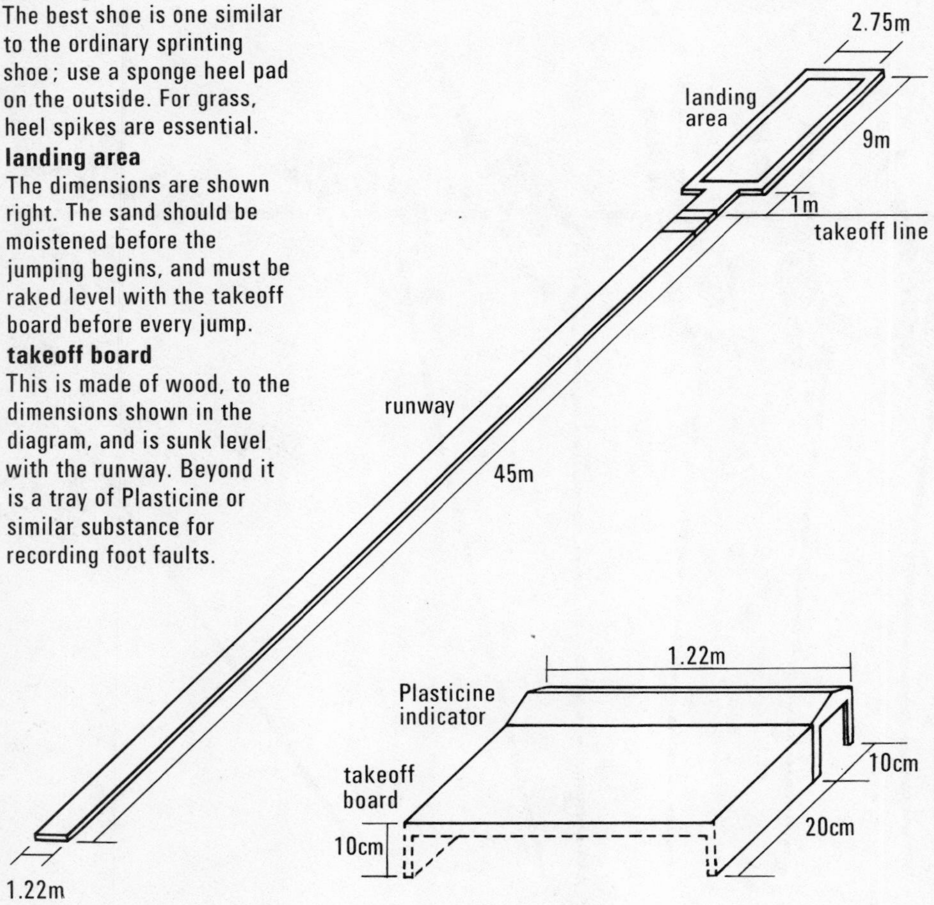

2.75m

landing area

9m

1m

takeoff line

runway

45m

1.22m

1.22m

Plasticine indicator

takeoff board

10cm

10cm

20cm

judging
There are four judges, who watch for failures, mark and measure the jumps, call up competitors, and clear the runway.

run-up
The length of the run-up is unlimited. Marks may be placed alongside, but not on, the runway; marks may not be placed beyond the takeoff line.

takeoff
The competitor should take off from the takeoff board itself (**a**). If he takes off earlier (**b**) it is not counted as a failure, but if he touches any part of the ground beyond the takeoff line (**c**) the jump is a failure. (This applies whether he makes his jump or only the run.) Weights or grips may not be used.

landing
It is a failure if a competitor, when landing, touches the ground outside the landing area nearer to the takeoff than the nearest break made by any part of his body in the landing area.

measurement
A jump is measured from the nearest break in the landing area made by any part of the competitor's body; measurement is up to the takeoff line and at right angles to it. Distances are recorded to the nearest 1cm (¼in) below the distance jumped.

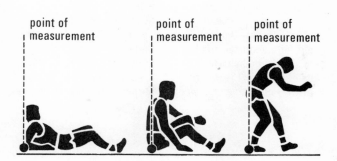

point of measurement

point of measurement

point of measurement

starting

There are various ways of
starting a run-up. A
standing start can be made
with the feet together or
with the feet apart; a
moving start can be made
by walking or jogging onto
the starting mark. The
normal length for a walking
or jogging start is 4
strides up to the starting
mark. Whichever method
you choose, the first stride
after the mark should be
with your takeoff leg.

finding your approach run

There are two ways of
doing this. One way is to
check the distance that you
cover in a certain number of
strides; run through this
distance six times, then try
it out on the runway and
attempt to jump. A friend,
counting each second stride,
can check the stride length.
Or you can start from the
takeoff board and run back,
letting a friend check the
final footmark; starting
from this point you run back
and jump.

approach run

The approach run is an
extremely important part of
the long jump. Most
top jumpers use an
approach run of 19–21
strides – a distance of
110–130ft (33–40m) –
but for a beginner it is best
to start with a shorter run-
up of perhaps 13–15 strides.
Always use an odd number
so that you start and take
off on the same foot.
Basically the approach run
consists of a build up of
speed, a fast middle run,
and then, about 5 strides
away from the takeoff
board, the preparation for
takeoff. The first strides
are in the style of a sprint,
(**1**) but during the last few
strides there is a change in
running action; the body
becomes more erect (**2**), the
knees are picked up higher
(**3,4**), and leg movement
becomes more rapid. At the
same time, 2 or 3
strides from takeoff, the
body is lowered and sinks
from the hips (**5,6**).

check and cue marks

A training shoe is usually used as a check mark. It is placed at the side of the runway so that you can see whether your foot lands opposite, and therefore whether your approach run is accurate. A first check mark is normally placed 3 strides out, and a second one about 7 strides from the board. A cue mark serves a different purpose; this is to remind you not to slacken speed as you approach the takeoff board.

takeoff

By takeoff you have reached your maximum speed, and your body should have lowered to allow for a good spring from the board (**7**). Now lift your free leg and ''strike'' the board with your takeoff foot as force-fully as possible (**8**). Your body should be absolutely erect, chest lifted right up.

Once in the air there is little you can do to gain momentum. The free leg is swung back and down (**9**), arms are swung back, round, over (**10**) and forward (**11**) in preparation for landing.

landing

Once you start dropping down you form a tucked position in the air (**12**), arms forward. As you land, legs should be outstretched as the heels strike the sand (**13**). The arms should be thrown backward immediately before landing, and then thrown forward.

flight

For beginners the flight is the least important aspect of the long jump, approach and takeoff needing more emphasis. But a good technique does help to control flight and to prepare efficiently for landing, and there are various flight techniques, the most commonly used being the Hang and Hitch-kick styles.

Hang

The Hang is fairly easy to learn and is used by both novices and experts.
1 Drive hard off the board.
2 Bend leading leg while bringing opposite arm up.
3 Bring arms back.
4 Straighten legs so that arms and legs trail behind in the classic "hang" position.
5 Throw arms up and round.

6 Bring knees up and arms forward.
7 Bring arms back as heels hit the sand.

Knee-tuck (Sail)

This technique is used only by beginners.
1 Take off from the board.
2 Bring takeoff leg up, keeping knees bent.
3 Tuck knees up toward chest.
4 Stretch arms out and start to extend legs for landing.
5 Bring arms back as heels touch the ground.

6 Land, knees bent, in a crouched position.
7 Let body fall forward, arms outstretched and palms down.

1   2

Hitch-kick

This is used, in one form or another, by most experts. In effect it is an airborne stride.
1 Drive off from the board; lift right knee high.
2, 3 Kick left leg out straight.
4 Sweep left leg down and back, and bring right knee up.
5 Kick left leg back and straighten right leg.
6, 7 Shoot both legs out to the front, and land.

1   2

Triple jump

The triple jump originated in Scotland and Ireland during the 19th century. It was taken to the United States, and in 1896 the first Olympic triple jump event was won by an Irish-American, James B. Connolly. The triple jump consists of a hop, step and jump sequence. In competition, the winner is the person with the best distance, usually after six tries.

jumping area
The dimensions are shown
in the diagram. The landing
area and takeoff board are
the same as for the long
jump, but for the triple jump
in international competitions
there must be 13m (43ft)
between them.
jumping action
Long jump rules apply for
run-up, initial takeoff,
landing and measuring.
Other rules are concerned
with the hop, step and jump
actions themselves.
For the hop the competitor
must land on the foot from
which he first took off; for
the step he must land on the
other foot. It is a failure if
he touches the ground with
his "sleeping" leg at any
point during the triple jump
action.
judging
There are five judges who
watch for failures, mark and
measure the jump, watch the
competitors' feet, and call
up competitors.

shoes
Heel spikes are
recommended for grass.
Plastic heel cups may also
be worn to protect the heel
bones.

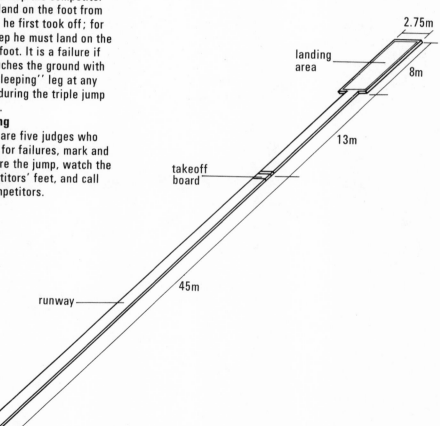

2.75m

landing area

8m

13m

takeoff board

45m

runway

1.22m

1

2   **3**

approach run
The approach run for triple jump is the same as for the long jump; again it is advisable for beginners to start with a short run-up of perhaps 3 strides.

beginners
To get the idea of the sequence, start with a standing triple jump from about 16ft (5m) from the landing area.
1,2 Hop from your right leg, holding your left leg behind you so that you land on your right foot.
3 Jump forward from your right foot.

4 Land on your left foot.
5 Jump from the left foot.
6 Stretch your legs out and your arms back.
7 Land.
Once you have mastered this, start again from a 3-stride approach.

1   **2**   **3**   **4**   **5**   **6**

triple jump sequence
1 Run onto board.
2 Striking the board down and back, take off from right foot.
3 Bring takeoff leg forward and arms up, keeping body erect.
4 Stretch right leg out to land; lower arms.

5 Land on right foot, heel first.
6 Drive off again.
7 Swing free leg up and forward; bring arms forward at the same time.
8 Bringing arms down, land on left foot.
9 Push off almost simultaneously from left foot.

10 Bringing free leg up and forward, stretch arms out ready for landing.
11 Swing arms down and back as feet hit sand.

4 **5** **6** **7**

basic points

Good balance is vital for the triple jump. To avoid toppling over at each landing you must land flat-footed and keep your body upright. The most crucial factor, however, is the rhythm and spacing that you develop. A common mistake at the beginning is to take a huge hop, a short recovery step, and a longer jump; basically you want to establish an even ta-ta-ta rhythm. To do this, practice with evenly-spaced check marks. With sand, mark out 7m (23ft) from the pit as a takeoff point. Put out pegs at 3m (10ft), 6m (20ft) and 7m (23ft). From a 3-stride approach aim to hit these marks accurately. Once you have developed an even rhythm, start extending the distances. Ultimately the type of spacing ratio you are aiming for is about 4:3:4.

7 **8** **9** **10** **11**

technique

One of the main points to remember is that, although the approach run is similar to that of the long jump, the takeoff is quite different. For the triple jump, taking off is much more of a running action, the leg striking down and back quite vigorously. The leg you choose for the initial takeoff is a matter of personal preference; because this leg has to be used twice (for the hop and the step) most people prefer to use their stronger leg, but others feel that this should be saved for the final takeoff (the jump). The best flight technique to use for the final jump is probably the Knee-tuck or Sail as it is the fastest and simplest, but the Hitch-kick and Hang are also used.

Jumping training

For all the jumping events, the training goals are much the same—overall physical fitness, muscular mobility and suppleness, and technical skill. Training programs should include running, weight training, and technique work.

high jump

Most people today prefer to use the Straddle or Fosbury Flop; their technical details have been shown previously. When practicing the Straddle the points to concentrate on are the approach run, take-off, and clearance. Start with a 3-stride approach, and, if you are a beginner, practice over a low bar held by a partner before graduating to a proper bar. Work on your free leg swing, back lean, and bar clearance. For the Fosbury Flop you can start with a Scissors jump from a short curving approach. Turn in the air to get used to landing on your back. Practice hollowing your back and lifting your hips.

long jump

For this event the points to watch for are a fast takeoff, a strong upward spring off the board, and a good landing. General training should include weight training, running, and mobility work, but from a technical point of view most of the training emphasis will be on getting a good, high spring off the board. You can practice this from a short approach run of 5–7 strides. Concentrate on driving yourself upward, and keeping your free knee high.

triple jump

Training for this event, as for all the jumps, includes sprinting, weight training, hopping and bounding, and strength and mobility exercises. Much work can be done indoors, in the form of depth jumping (below); this consists of hopping and bounding onto and over boxes and bars. The variations and permutations of jumps are virtually endless. The boxes should be between 19–31in (50–80cm) high and the training is best done in a gym.

pole vault

For this event training includes sprinting (with or without a pole), vaulting, strength training, and general gymnastics. Agility is essential, as are strong shoulders. Hand walking, hand stands, push ups, and rope climbing are good ways of achieving both.

exercises

All warming-up exercises are good for increasing your mobility and for toning up your muscles and joints. For muscle strength, which is needed particularly by pole vaulters in the shoulders and arms, a simple weight training routine can be followed. If you are inexperienced, use light weights to begin with, under supervision, and increase the weight as you progress.

running

Apart from sprinting, some time should be devoted to interval running and fartlek. In the first you run for several fast bursts with a recovery period between the bursts; in the second you run at varying speeds without timing yourself.

There are four throwing events—javelin, discus, hammer and shot put. As with all sporting events, their origins are ancient, and fairly obscure. Javelin and discus throwing were both practiced by the ancient Greeks; discus throwing was the most popular of all their sports and was one of the five events in their pentathlon. Javelin throwing is probably the oldest field event still practiced in virtually its original form. The main difference between the ancient Greek javelin thrower and his modern counterpart is that the former probably used a leather thong or strap as a throwing aid.

The origins of the hammer and shot put are completely lost. The first hammer contests may have been between ancient Celtic tribes in Britain; as a formal event, hammer throwing was first recognized in 1866. The modern shot event evolved from a 12th century event known as "casting the stone;" much later, stone throwing was practiced as a formal event at the Tailteann Games in Ireland in 1829. The shot itself was standardized in about 1850. No matter what their origins, these events are becoming increasingly popular. With the exception of javelin throwing, some of them have long been thought of as only suitable for the heavy, tough men of athletics, but in fact only one throwing event—the hammer—is confined to men. All the throwing events are highly-skilled and thrilling to watch. Perfection in any one of them takes years, but they have the added attraction of being enjoyable at any level of skill.

After an approach run, the javelin is thrown from behind a curved line and must land, point first, within the marked sector. In competition each athlete has three or six trials; the competitor with the longest throw is the winner. Because javelins are so long, and are pointed at both ends, safety precautions must be observed when carrying them as well as when throwing.

shoes
The best shoes to wear are those with heel and sole spikes; you can have up to six sole and two heel spikes, but not more.

javelin
A javelin can be made of wood, steel, or wood and alloy. It must have no moving parts. A cord grip is bound around its center of gravity but the circumference of the binding must not exceed that of the shaft by more than 25mm (1in). The length and weight of a javelin varies depending on whether it is for a man, a woman, or a junior athlete. The minimum weight for men is 800g (1lb 12.2oz) and for women and boys 600g·(1lb 5.16oz).

throwing action
The javelin must be held at the grip or binding and must be neither slung nor hurled. It must be thrown over the shoulder or upper part of the throwing arm. During the throw the competitor is not allowed to turn completely around. It is a foul if the competitor touches the arc, the scratch lines, or the ground beyond them with any part of his body. The parallel lines must not be crossed. The competitor must not leave the delivery area until the javelin has landed, when he must leave from behind the arc and scratch lines.

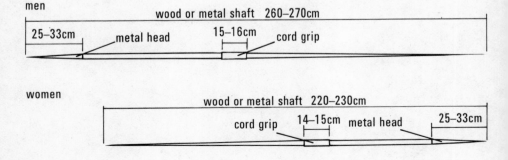

men

wood or metal shaft   260–270cm

25–33cm   metal head   15–16cm   cord grip

women

wood or metal shaft   220–230cm

cord grip   14–15cm   metal head   25–33cm

practice throws

You can practice in the arena before any throwing event, but only from or near the circles or scratch line. For safety, javelins must always be returned by hand whether you are practicing or in competition.

landing

The javelin must land, tip first, within the inner edge of the sector lines. It need not stick into the ground.

broken javelin

If the javelin breaks in the air, the trial is not counted provided all the rules have been observed.

judging

A white flag is used for a fair throw, and a red one for a foul. Judge (**a**) watches whether the competitor touches or crosses the arc or scratch line. Judge (**b**) watches the approach and the way the javelin is held. Judges (**c**) and (**d**) watch the landing of the javelin.

measurement

A throw is measured from the nearest mark made by the head of the javelin to the inner edge of the circumference of the arc. Measurement is along a line from the mark and through the center of the radius of the arc.

the arc

The arc is of wood or metal, painted white and sunk flush with the ground, or it may be simply a painted white line.

sector flags

These are used to mark the outer ends of the sector.

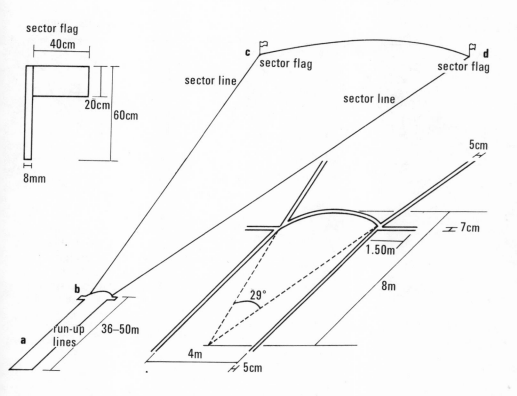

1   **2**   **3**   **4**   **5**

grip

There are three basic ways of gripping the javelin:

a between thumb and index finger

b between thumb and middle finger

c between index and middle finger; this "horseshoe" or "claw" grip is probably the most effective.

In all methods the javelin must always be held firmly and must run down the length of the palm, not across it.

approach run

The approach run is divided into two phases: the preliminary run-up and what is sometimes called the transition phase.

preliminary run-up

1 Stand with your feet together, carrying the javelin in the way that you find most comfortable and easiest to run with. In general it is best carried parallel to the ground, above the throwing shoulder. Your elbow should be bent forward. Start running on your right foot. The length

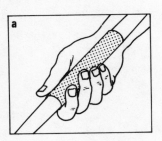

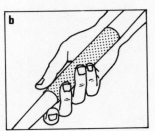

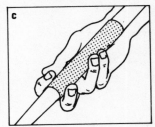

practice

You can practice the javelin action quite simply. Place a marker about 15ft (5m) away. Grip the javelin, draw it well back close to your face and "stab" it hard at the marker.

6   **7**   **8**   **9**

of the preliminary run varies from 4–12 strides. As a beginner, start with a short run-up. During this part of the approach, keep the javelin above your shoulder and aim for a smooth, gradual build-up of speed.

transition phase

This phase takes up 5 strides, and no matter what the length of the preliminary run-up, it is these 5 strides that are the most vital. During these the javelin and your body are moved into position for the throw. Use a check mark as a reminder to move into this phase.

2 Hit the check mark with your right foot; bring your left leg through.

3 As you land on your left foot, begin to pull the javelin back and turn your shoulders slightly to the side. Keep your hips facing forward; take off from your left leg.

4 Bringing the right leg through, pick your right knee up high so that it crosses your left leg virtually in mid-stride.

5 Land on your right foot, heel first so that your body leans backward.

6 Bend your right knee.

the throw

7 Stride onto your left leg, ready to throw.

8 Arch your back, drive your right hip forward and upward.

9 Pull your right arm over your shoulder, keep your elbow high, and throw the javelin.

Finnish-style

For many years the Finns dominated the javelin event at the Olympics—Matti Jarvinen was probably one of the greatest javelin throwers of all time. Even today the major record holders are still Scandinavian, and as a result the Finnish method of approach and delivery, shown here, has been adopted by many international athletes.

1 Hit your check mark (5 strides from the arc) with your left foot.

2 Run onto your right foot, which should be pointing straight ahead.

3 Move onto your left foot so that it points slightly to the right; straighten your throwing arm so that the javelin is parallel to the ground.

4 Stride onto your right foot, moving foot, leg and hip round to the right; pull javelin back.

5 Land on your right foot, bring your left foot forward; lean back.

6 Take a long stride onto your left leg; pull the

angle of release

In javelin throwing you need to concentrate on three main things: a fast throwing action, a stable release, and the best possible angle of release. In general you should try to throw the javelin at an angle of between 30–40° from the ground.

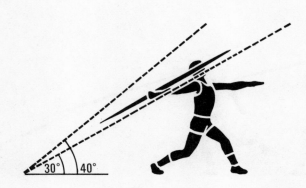

javelin through.
7 Bring your elbow forward.
8 Throw.
9 Straighten your right arm.
10 Land on your right foot close to the arc; to recover your balance, hop on your right foot, stretching your left leg back and out to the side. Use your arms to balance yourself.

For this version you should grip the javelin behind the binding between your second finger and thumb, so that your second finger virtually encircles the shaft. During the preliminary run-up hold the javelin to the front of your body, point well down. Move the javelin up and down as you run so that the movements of your throwing arm synchronize with the movements of your opposite leg.

specific training
1 Thread a weighted rope through a pulley about 12ft (3.6m) above the floor. Fix the cord grip of a javelin to the free end. Stand on a box and, holding the grip, practice your throwing action.

2 Use the same pulley system; this time grip the rope with both hands and, using your lower back, concentrate on arching your back and driving your hips forward in the "bow" position.

Hammer throwing destroys carefully nurtured turf and as a result this highly-skilled event tends to be neglected, particularly in schools. Of all the throwing events, it is the most technically complex. The aim is to release the hammer, at the maximum possible speed, at an angle of about 40°. The hammer must be thrown from within a circle to land within a marked sector. To build up speed the thrower turns, and it is this turning that calls for a great deal of skill.

hammer glove
A right-handed thrower usually wears a protective glove on his left hand. There are also special hammer shoes but any flat-soled gym shoes are suitable.

11cm

10.5cm   117.5–121.5cm   102–120mm

hammer
The hammer head can be of any metal not softer than brass, or it can be a shell of this metal filled with such material as lead. The head is attached by a swivel to the handle, which is a single length of steel wire with a 3mm (⅛in) diameter. The grip can be a single or double loop without hinged joints. The minimum weight for a complete hammer is 7.26kg (16lb).

cage
For safety reasons in competitions the throwing circle for the hammer and discus is always shielded by a metal cage. In training, if there is no cage available, no-one should stand within throwing distance.

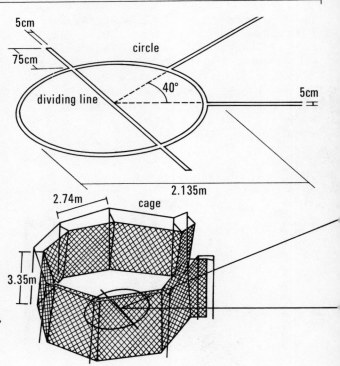

5cm

circle

75cm

40°

dividing line

5cm

2.135m

2.74m   cage

3.35m

measurement

A throw is measured from the nearest mark made by the head of the hammer to the inner edge of the ring bounding the circle. Measurement is along a line from the mark and through the center of the circle. Distances are recorded to the nearest 2cm (1in) below the distance thrown.

interrupting a trial

A competitor is allowed one interruption for each trial, but he must not interrupt a trial in which the hammer head has touched the ground during the preliminary swings or turns.

landing

The hammer must land within the inner edge of the sector lines.

judging

There are normally five judges for this event. Positions and responsibilities are as for discus throwing.

throwing action

The competitor must begin his throw from a stationary position, when he is permitted to rest the head of the hammer on the ground inside or outside the circle. The hammer head may also touch the ground during preliminary turns or swings (**a**).

A throw is a foul if, after starting his action, the competitor touches with any part of his body either the top of the ring bounding the circle or the ground beyond it (**b**).

The competitor must not leave the circle until the hammer has landed, when he must, from a standing position, leave from behind the dividing line.

broken hammer

A trial is not counted if the hammer breaks during throwing or flight, provided the throw was made in accordance with the rules. Nor is it counted a foul if the broken hammer causes the competitor to lose his balance and so infringe the rules.

a

b

sector flag

sector line

sector line

sector flag

the grip

Grip the handle with your left hand, placing your right hand over your left fingers. (The grip shown here and the following sequences are for right-handed throwers.)

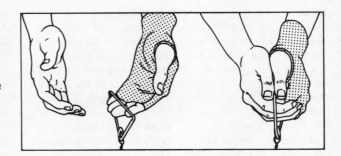

practice swings

1 Stand with your feet comfortably apart, hammer lying behind your right foot, wire fully stretched.
2 Swing the hammer in a circular motion, bending your arms so that your hands pass close to your forehead.
3 Straighten your arms as the hammer passes your right knee.

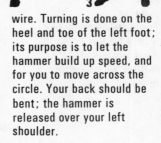

preliminary swings

To get the hammer into motion before turning with it, you give it two or three preliminary swings. The hammer should move in a wide, loose arc, forward and up; don't try to influence its motion but keep your arms straight and relaxed, bending them only as they move overhead.

fundamentals

Learn to do a two-turn throw, shown below, before trying the more usual three turns. As the hammer rises you move straight from your second swing into your first turn. The main point to remember is to keep your arms straight throughout— think of them as an extension of the hammer wire. Turning is done on the heel and toe of the left foot; its purpose is to let the hammer build up speed, and for you to move across the circle. Your back should be bent; the hammer is released over your left shoulder.

preliminary swings   start of turn

"stutter" turns

To get the feel of turning, practice a few so-called "stutter" turns. Swing the hammer twice (**a**) then, letting the hammer lead you (**b**), turn yourself with tiny "stuttering" steps along a straight line. Watch the hammer head, keeping your arms and back straight and your knees bent.

the turn

This is the hardest part of the throw to master. The diagram shows the footwork for one single turn.

1 Start with your back to the direction of the throw. Turn on the heel, then toe, of the left foot, shifting your weight over your left leg. As your left foot turns, pick up your right leg, the right hip forcing the body into a complete turn. The right foot turns on the toe. You should turn as the hammer swings up so that both your feet are on the ground as it swings down.

2 End your turn in the same position as you started, but further across the circle.

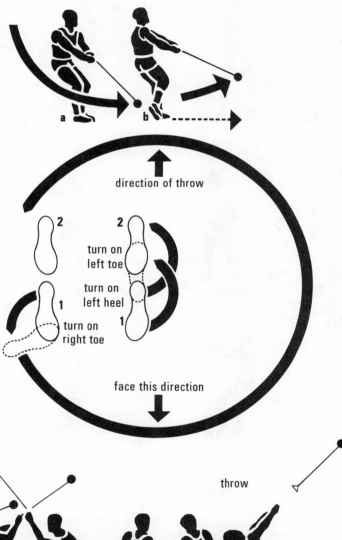

direction of throw

turn on
left toe

turn on
left heel

turn on
right toe

face this direction

second turn

throw

three turns: footwork
1 Start facing away from the direction of your throw.
2 Begin turning on the heel of your left foot; raise your right foot onto its toes.
3 Continue turning on the outside edge of the ball of your left foot.
4 Keeping your thighs close together, lift your right foot.
5 Still turning on your left

foot, bring your right hip round.
6 Continue turning on the toes of your left foot and bring your right foot back to the ground to complete one turn.
7 Again start your second turn
8 on the heel of your left foot.
9 Pick your right foot up.

10 Turn on your left foot, bringing your right hip round.
11 Bring your right foot back to the ground.
12 Complete the second turn.
13 Turn for the third time on your left heel and lift your right foot off the ground.
14 Bring your right leg through.

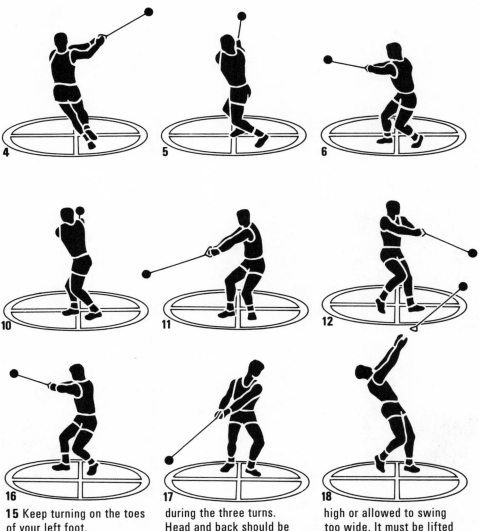

15 Keep turning on the toes of your left foot.
16 Bring your right foot back to the ground.
17 Complete your third turn and
18 release the hammer.
For a beginner the main problem is loss of balance. To avoid toppling over you must keep your body weight mainly over your left foot

during the three turns. Head and back should be kept upright, and the legs bent. Physical effort comes from the hips, legs and feet. The left foot does the bulk of the work, turning on its heel for about half the turn and on the outside edge of the ball of the foot for the other half. The right foot must not be picked up too

high or allowed to swing too wide. It must be lifted just enough to get it off the ground and round the left leg.
Your first turn should be fairly slow, your speed building up until you reach maximum speed in the third turn. With each turn the hammer will move faster.

three-turn sequence
1 Stand with your feet apart at the rear of the circle, your back to the direction of the throw.
2 Swing the hammer forward; grip the handle in your gloved left hand; enclose your left hand in your right palm.
3 Swing the hammer back and

4 forward; shift your weight to the left.
5 Shift your weight to the right and keep your arms straight as the hammer swings low.
6 Swing the hammer round and forward,
7 bending your arms as it comes round behind your head and over your shoulder.

8 Swing the hammer through and shift your weight to the left.
9 Go into your first turn.
10 Turn on your left heel.
11 Pick your right foot up; keep your arms straight and your knees bent.
12 Twist your hips round.
13 Complete the turn.
14 Start to turn again on your left heel.

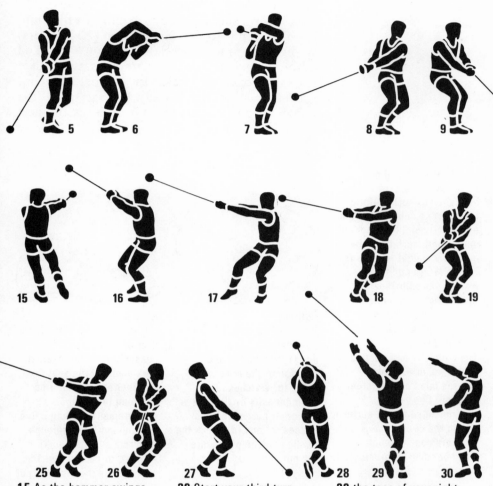

15 As the hammer swings up, pick up your right foot.
16 Turn on the ball of your left foot.
17 Keep your weight over your left foot to counter-balance the pull of the hammer.
18 Bring your right foot back to the ground.
19 Complete the second turn.

20 Start your third turn.
21 Twist round on your left heel.
22 Pick your right foot up.
23 Keep turning on
24 the toes of your left foot.
25 Bring your right foot down, keeping your weight over your left foot; complete the third turn.
26 Keep your knees bent;
27 turn on your left heel and

28 the toes of your right foot; "lift" the hammer.
29 Release it over your left shoulder.
30 Recover.
training
Hammer throwing requires a great deal of stamina and strength; training should include regular weight and resistance work to improve both qualities.

The main point about shot putting is that the shot is not thrown. In effect the shot is "pushed" from the shoulder, and, to avoid throwing it, must always stay in close proximity to the chin. The shot is put from a circle 7 feet (2.13 meters) in diameter and must land within a marked sector. To give the put extra impetus, the athlete moves across the circle. In competitive shot putting each athlete usually has six trials, the winner being the person who achieves the best distance.

the shot
This is made of solid iron, brass, or any metal not softer than brass, or it can be a shell of such material filled with a substance such as lead. It must be spherical and smooth-surfaced. The minimum weight for men is 7.26kg (16lb) and for women 4kg (8lb 13oz). Shot weights for juniors vary with age. Shoes without spikes are worn.

the circle
The boundary is a painted white line or a white-painted band of iron, steel or wood. Concrete is recommended for the surface within the circle. There is also a raised stopboard of wood or some other material.

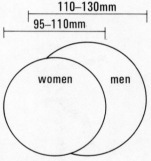

judging
A white flag indicates a fair throw and a red flag a foul. Judge (**a**) watches the position of the arms and judge (**b**) watches for infringements by the foot or any other part of the body. Judges (**c**) and (**d**) check the landing and help measure the put.

measurement
This takes place immediately after each trial. Puts are measured from the nearest mark made by the shot to the inner edge of the ring bounding the circle. Measurement is along a line from the mark and through the circle's center, and is recorded to the nearest 1cm (¼in) below the distance put.

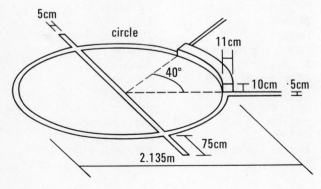

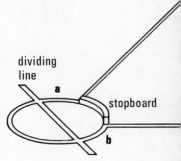

putting action

The competitor must begin his put from a stationary position. Only one hand may be used, and throughout the putting action this hand must not drop below its starting position. The shot must not be brought in front of the shoulder line.
A put is invalid if the competitor, after com-mencing his action, touches with any part of his body the top of the stopboard (**a**) or the ring bounding the circle, or the ground outside (**b**). He is allowed to touch the inside of the stopboard or ring. The competitor must not leave the circle until the shot has landed; he must then, standing, leave from behind the dividing line.

interrupting a trial

Provided there has been no infringement, a competitor is allowed one interruption for each trial. When interrupting a trial, the competitor may lay down his shot; he must then restart from a stationary position.

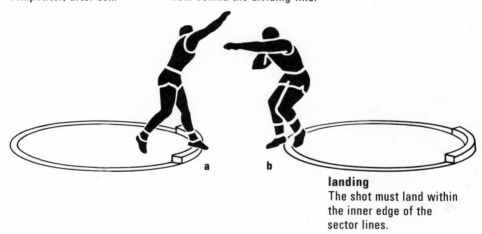

a   b

landing

The shot must land within the inner edge of the sector lines.

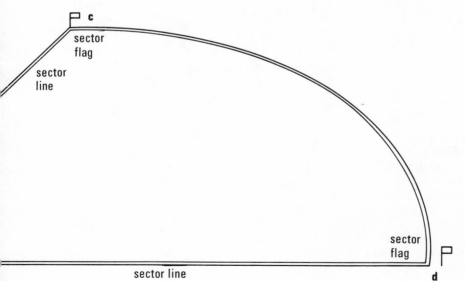

c

sector flag

sector line

sector flag

d

sector line

grip

The shot should be held at the base of the three middle fingers. (At first you will find it easiest to carry the shot low in the palm; as you get more experienced the shot should be held further toward the fingertips.) The thumb and little finger support the shot; the little finger can be either bent (**a**) or straight (**b**). For those with short, stubby fingers, it is best to move the little finger next to the other three at the back of the shot (**c**).

The second hold (**b**) is the most effective; the little finger not only helps to balance the shot but also helps to propel it.

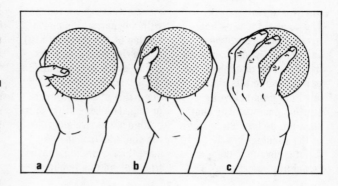

carrying the shot

The shot should be pressed well into the neck, resting in the hollow where the collarbone meets the neck. Your wrist should press under the shot, elbow well out. During your put, "chase" the shot out as far as possible with your elbow and hand.

standing put

To get the correct arm action, you can practice putting the shot from a standing position.

1 Stand with your feet hip-width apart; hold the shot well into your neck, keeping your right elbow out and left arm up.

2 Turn slightly to the right; bring your left arm across your body.

3 Bring your left arm back rapidly, keep your legs straight, and "push" the shot forward.

4 Follow it through with your right arm.

Keep your throwing elbow out and away from your body throughout.

leg drive

Shot putting is a sequence of movements which should flow smoothly into one another. The put is made by driving with your legs. The hips turn first, the right hip lifting up and driving forward. The shoulders follow, and then the arm pushes and chases the shot through.

trunk twist

To get real distance you must use the powerful muscles of your trunk and legs. Practice by starting low over your right leg. Twist your trunk round and push the shot hard away from you.

moving across the circle

Once you've mastered the standing put you need to practice moving across the circle. It is the preliminary movements across the circle that help to give the shot extra momentum. The sequence above shows a very simple "cross-step" technique which you can start with.

1 Stand at the rear of the circle, the shot tucked well into your neck.
2 Lean your weight over your left leg.
3 Pick your right foot up and cross it over your left.
4 As your right foot lands, stretch your left leg over to the stop board; lean over to the right.

5 Drive your right hip forward and put the shot.

side-on technique
1 Stand at the rear of the
circle, shot tucked well into
your neck; bend forward,
lift your left leg up, and in.
2 Move your left leg out;
flex your right leg and shift
it to the center of the circle.
3 Bring your left leg down
by the stop board; drive
forward with your right hip,

4 and push the shot away
from you.
Essentially this movement is
a glide across the circle.
Make sure that you do not
straighten up as you move
across, but keep your
weight over your right foot.

the O'Brien shift
This is the technique used
by virtually all top-class shot
putters today.
1 Stand at the rear of the
circle with your back to the
direction of the put; place
your right foot against the
rear edge of the circle, your
left a short distance behind.
2 Bend forward from the
hips; raise your left leg and

bring your left thigh into
your right leg.
3 Shoot your left leg up and
4 back toward the stop
board; drive off from your
right heel.
5 Flex your right knee,
shifting your right foot to
the center of the circle;
land with your left foot at
the stop board.
6 Swing your left arm out.

7 Drive your right hip round
and forward so that your
body rotates.
8 Bring your shoulders
round, lift your hips, and
9 put the shot.
10 Follow through, swinging
your right foot against the
stop board; swing your left
leg back and up to keep
your balance.

step-back technique
This is slightly more
advanced.
1 Start at the rear of the
circle, your back to the
direction of the put; bend
your left leg and stretch
your right leg back.
2 Pick your left leg up, and
3 step back to the stop
board.

4 Drive your right hip round
and forward and ''chase''
the shot away with your
right arm.

the glide
As you move across the
circle your right foot should
only just break contact with
the ground. As you move
through the air your right
foot is turned in and to the
right, so that you can then
drive your hip into the
put effectively. At the same
time the left hip moves
across and to the left. Your

left foot should land in line
with the heel of the right
foot, close to the stopboard.

training
Most shot putters are strong,
and usually quite heavy. The
event calls for speed,
suppleness and strength. A
typical training program
should include jogging,
sprinting, hurdling, weight
training and suppleness
exercises, particularly for
the arms, shoulders and
back.

Discus throwing is a skilled event, the skill lying in the athlete's ability to "flight" the discus correctly. The discus is thrown from within a circle and must land in the marked sector. In competition, depending on the number of athletes, competitors have between three and six trials; the winner is the athlete with the best distance. Discus throwing is dangerous, and safety rules must be observed: only throw from the circle, and only throw in the set direction.

the discus
The discus is made of wood or other suitable material, and is bound by a smooth metal rim. A weight is secured in the center of the discus. Minimum discus weights are 2kg (4lb 6.54oz) for men, 1kg (2lb 3.25oz) for women and girls, and 1.25kg (2lb 10.8oz) for boys.

the circle
The discus is thrown from a circle bounded by a white line or a white-painted band of iron, steel or wood. There is no stopboard for the discus circle.

men   219–221mm

44–46mm

37–39mm

women   180–182mm

5cm

75cm

dividing line

40°

5cm

circle

2.50m

position on the field
Discus and hammer events are generally held in the same area so that only one safety cage is needed.

2.74m

a   cage

sector line

c

3.35m

b

holding the discus
The most usual method is
illustrated. Fingers must not
be taped together.
shoes
Shoes without spikes are
worn for discus events.

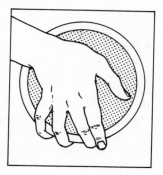

throwing action
The competitor must begin
his throw from a stationary
position. He may hold the
discus as he wishes and use
any throwing technique. His
throw is a foul if, after
beginning his action, he
touches with any part of his
body either the top of the
ring bounding the circle or
the ground beyond it; this
rule remains in force while
the discus is in flight.
At the end of the throw the
competitor must, from a
standing position, leave the
circle from behind the
dividing line.

interrupting a trial
Provided there has been no
infringement a competitor is
allowed one interruption for
each trial. When interrupting
a trial, the competitor may
lay down his discus; he
must then recommence his
action from a stationary
position.
judging
Five judges are needed.
Judges (**a**) and (**b**) watch on
their own side for infringements within the circle.
(Their positions are
reversed for left-handed
throwers.) Three judges are
needed in the field since
the landing area is
unpredictable (**c,d,e**).

landing
The discus must land
within the inner edge of the
sector lines.
measurement
A throw is measured from
the nearest mark made by
the discus to the inner edge
of the ring bounding the
circle. Measurement is
along a line from the mark
and through the center of
the circle. Distances are
recorded to the nearest 2cm
(1in) below the distance
thrown.

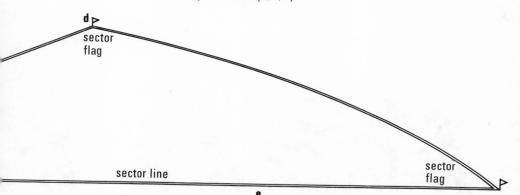

d ▷
sector
flag

sector line

sector
flag ▷

e

Discus basics

The discus throw is essentially a long slinging action in which the propelling arm is kept as straight as possible. As the discus is released it is spun to stabilize its flight; for extra speed the athlete starts the throw with a running turn across the circle. Before attempting the complete throw, master the hold, spin and throw from a standing position. For safety always use a specific throwing area, throw in one direction only, and only retrieve your discus when everyone has finished throwing.

throwing
The discus is held rather than gripped; it should rest against the palm of the hand, fingers just curling over the edge. As it is released it should be finger spun so that it goes through the air as flat as possible; if it presents too large a surface to air resistance its flight will be killed. Practice by spinning the discus across the ground.

learning to throw
These stages will help you to master the correct throwing action.
First, practice easy, low swings with the discus. Then make some swings at shoulder level. Next, stoop down after the swing and spin the discus out. When you feel confident, try some standing throws, and then try turning slightly into the throw. Finally, make a slow complete turn before the discus is released.

standing throw
Start with the discus by your left shoulder, supported in your left hand and covered by your right. Step back onto the toes of your right foot and draw the discus back as far as possible in your right hand. Drive your right hip foward, putting your weight onto your left leg, and spin the discus out.

balance
Good balance is an essential part of a successful throw, as it ensures that the athlete is in full control of the movement across the circle and the release of the discus. Preliminary swings must not be too large or too vigorous, as they may cause balance problems. During the turn, avoid wide sweeping movements as these tend to change the axis of rotation and make the turn unpredictable.

leg and hip action
The right hip plays an important part in the discus movement. Throughout the turn and the throw you should feel as though you are constantly forcing the hip to the front, in order to increase the power and speed of the release. The left leg should act as a brace to the fast-moving right side, but it should not be kept rigid or it will impede the body's movement.

arm action
The arm is used to complete the throwing action that the body has begun. Timing is vital here; if the arm movement begins too early, it meets resistance from the left shoulder. Most of the arm movement should take place when the chest is square to the front.

1½ turn sequence

1 Stand side-on to the direction of the throw: draw the discus back.

2 Set your left toe in the direction of your turn.

3 Bring your right knee up in a running motion, and start the turn on your left foot.

4 Keep your right arm straight; look over your left shoulder.

5 Bring your right foot down and

6 turn on your right foot.

7 Bring your left leg round and

8 to the ground; rotate your body to the left, trailing your throwing arm.

9 Drive your right hip forward and upward.

10 Keep your head up; release the discus and follow it through with your right arm.

1¾ turn throw

1 Start at the rear of the circle. Swing the discus back; keep your left arm wrapped across your chest; move into the turn.

2 Turn, using your left leg as a pivot.

3 Continue turning; keep your weight over your left leg.

4 Complete the drive across the circle with your left leg.

5 Pick your right thigh up high.

6 Land on your right foot, knee bent.

7 Turn on your right foot.

8 Shoot your left leg toward the front of the circle.

9 Turn your right foot in and drive your hips round to the front.

10 Bring your shoulders round.
11 Straighten your left leg and
12 release the discus.

The turn is a running-type action involving one complete leg cycle. For right-handed throwers this means pivoting around the left foot, keeping the body weight over the left leg. In effect your right leg and hip rotate your body, and your left leg takes you across the circle in a straight line. You should start your movement across the circle slowly, and finish fast, ending at the front of the circle in a ''wound-up'' throwing position, hips ahead of your shoulders, throwing arm trailing behind.

training

There is no such thing as a universal training program —each individual must work out his or her personal training schedule, ideally with a coach or fellow athlete.

The throwing events are probably the most skilled of all athletic events, and with the exception of javelin throwing, tend to be for the strong, heavy athlete. In differing degrees of importance they all require gross or absolute strength, elastic strength (the ability of muscles to act fast during the event), mobility and, of course, skill. This means that apart from the conventional running and jumping activities, the thrower must concentrate on weight training, resistance training, mobility exercises, and technique training.

Skills can be broken down into simple drills and these drills, using assistance equipment such as pulleys or a medicine ball, should be practiced intensively. Warming up is vitally important. Each training session and each competitive event should be preceded by a warm-up session.

javelin throwing

The javelin thrower needs to be a good all-round athlete —in fact it has been said that a javelin thrower needs to be a good decathlete. The event demands a high degree of skill, mobility, and elastic strength. Training should include sprinting, hurdling, long-jumping, and

shot put

Strength is the first requirement for the shot putter, with skill and mobility also high on the list of priorities. During the winter the accent should be on strength training, with the athlete lifting the maximum amount of weight possible. Suitable lifts

discus

Strength, mobility, skill and speed are the main requirements for a discus thrower, and about 80% of training time should be directed toward achieving these. Weight training develops general strength. There are also a number of drills, which include the use of friction pulleys and

hammer

Hammer throwing needs strength, mobility and skill. Technique training and weight training can be combined using either a heavy hammer on a chain (**a**) or a 16lb (7.26kg) shot (**b**). Both of these can be used to exercise the legs and back and to practice delivery. To exercise the

weight training.

As for all throwers, training must include specific strength training. The drill shown here in which the medicine ball is thrown overhead with a double hand hold is good for strengthening and mobilizing the back muscles.

include the "clean" and "bench press." Weight training by itself can reduce muscle flexibility, and suppleness exercises must also be incorporated. The overhead throw shown here uses a medicine ball. The drill will help technique, and strengthen and mobilize your shoulders and trunk.

medicine balls, that can be used to develop specific strength and mobility relevant to this particular event. The drill shown here makes use of a medicine ball in the discus throwing action. It helps to improve technique, at the same time strengthening and flexing the relevant muscles.

legs, turn into a deep knee bend using a heavy hammer (**a**). To exercise the back muscles, grip the shot in both hands (**b**), swing down between your legs, then deliver it over your head.

Decathlon and pentathlon

Decathlon and pentathlon

The decathlon is an entirely modern event, but a pentathlon existed in the ancient Olympics; it was introduced in about 708BC and consisted of long jump, discus, sprint, javelin and wrestling. The scoring system was very simple; as soon as any athlete won three events he was declared the victor, and any remaining events were abandoned.

The first modern decathlon probably took place in Germany in 1911, but it was featured as an Olympic event for the first time in 1912. Then, as now, it consisted of 100m, long jump, shot, high jump, 400m, 110m hurdles, discus, pole vault, javelin, and 1500m; the pentathlon events, however, have changed since that time. The modern athletics pentathlon should not be confused with the so-called "modern pentathlon", which is an event involving riding, shooting, running, swimming and fencing.

The decathlon takes place over two days and is an event for men only; the pentathlon takes place over one or two days, and is for women only. In 1976 it was suggested that a heptathlon of seven events should be introduced for women.

decathlon day 1
a 100m
b Long jump
c Shot put
d High jump
e 400m

decathlon day 2
f 110m hurdles
g Discus
h Pole vault
i Javelin
j 1500m

decathlon events
The decathlon consists of ten events: 100m, long jump, shot put, high jump, 400m, 110m hurdles, discus, pole vault, javelin, and 1500m. The events must be held in the order listed; the first five are held on the first day, and the others on the second day.

rules
International Amateur Athletic Federation (IAAF) rules generally apply for each event. Exceptions are that competitors are allowed only three trials in each field event, and that three false starts in a track event result in an elimination without points from that event.

c

d

e

h

i

j

scoring
Points are awarded
according to the IAAF
scoring tables. They
are awarded for
performance. The winner is
the athlete who obtains the
highest total over the ten
events.

order of competing
This is drawn before each
event.

race draws
In most competitions below
international level, athletes
of similar standard are
usually placed in the same
heats for all track events
except the 1500m.

withdrawals
If a competitor fails to take
part in any event he must
withdraw from the entire
decathlon.

tie
If a tie occurs, the winner is
the athlete with the most
points in the majority of
events. If the tie remains,
the athlete with the most
points in any one event
wins.

pentathlon
a 100m hurdles
b Shot put
c High jump
d Long jump
e 800m

a

b

c

d

e

pentathlon events
The pentathlon consists of
five events: 100m hurdles,
shot put, high jump, long
jump, and 800m. The events
must be held in the order
listed, and preferably
should all take place on the
same day.

rules and scoring
The rules and scoring are
basically the same as for
the decathlon.

pointers

The decathlon and pentathlon are the two most grueling events on the athletics program. In particular the two-day decathlon, with its ten diverse components, is the absolute test of speed, skill, strength and stamina. Probably the best formula for a decathlete is to be a fast runner with good jumping ability.

Technical training depends on the athlete's individual qualities—it's good policy to concentrate on weak events while working ''little and often'' on stronger points. For beginners the 110m hurdles and the pole vault tend to be the hardest events. In the main, training policy is much the same for the pentathlete, although here speed is the prime requisite. Training should include running, hurdling, and plenty of shot put practice.

training and tactics

Training for one specific event is fairly straight-forward compared with training for the pentathlon and decathlon. For these an athlete has to master five or ten different events. There is no point in following a specialist program— instead aim for all-round competence, concentrating on your weakest points. Simplify each skill as much as possible into basic drills which can then be practiced. One international coach has said that the main tactic is ''living in the present, forgetting the past, and not anticipating the future.'' Concentrate on each event as it occurs, forgetting your past achievements or failures. The main aim is to score reasonably in each event; to some extent this means playing safe, particularly in the first jumping and throwing trials.

food

Before the contest you should eat a normal breakfast. During the contest Calories are burned up extremely rapidly, and you should eat high-carbohydrate snacks such as chocolate biscuits. Hot and cold drinks and a light, cold meal are usually provided, but you may prefer to avoid eating a meal; in this case you should use a milk-based food supplement.

equipment

Choose your equipment so that you are warm and well-prepared at all times. Top athletes need two pairs of spiked shoes, two pairs of gym shoes, two track suits, vests, shorts, and a parka. You should also have a Thermos for hot or cold drinks.

Cross-country events

Cross-country races are governed more by local conditions than detailed rules. Generally cross-country running is a winter sport in which individuals and teams run over courses through the countryside. The first runner to complete the course is the winner; team performances are determined by the aggregate placings of individual team members.

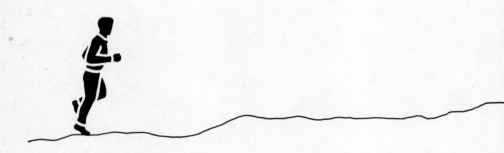

courses
For major events the course should be confined to open country, fields, heathland, and grassland. Roads should be avoided, and there should be no excessively difficult obstacles. Competitors should ideally be allowed an unrestricted run for the first 1400m (1 mile).

markings
The course should be clearly marked, with red flags on the left and white flags on the right.

distances
Senior men's distances should be at least 8km (5 miles); international races should be at least 12km (about 7 miles); national championships at least 14.5km (about 9 miles). Women's senior events should be between 2–5km (1¼–3¼ miles).

start
Races are started with a pistol shot. A 5-minute warning may be given if there are many competitors.

assistance
Competitors may not receive assistance or refreshment during a race.

team scoring
After the race the placings of the scoring members of each team are added together. The team with the best aggregate is the winner. If there is a tie, the team whose last scoring runner finished before the other team's last scoring runner is awarded the higher place.

officials
Officials for a major event should include a referee, a judge, a timekeeper, a starter, funnel judges and funnel controllers for the finish, result recorders, and assistants.

competitors
Runners may compete individually or in teams; a race may include both types of competition.

teams
In international events a team must have at least six and no more than nine runners, plus five reserves.

clothing
Studded running shoes or orienteering shoes are best for soft, wet courses. Running shorts may be worn with a long-sleeved singlet or sports jersey.

Orienteering is a fairly new and fast-growing sport, enjoyed by people of all ages. Individuals or teams navigate their way on foot around a course using a map, a compass, and their own initiative. There are four main types of orienteering—point (a straight race around a circuit of control points); relay, in which the circuits are completed by a team; line (where the complete route is marked out); and score orienteering, where as many controls as possible are visited in a given time.

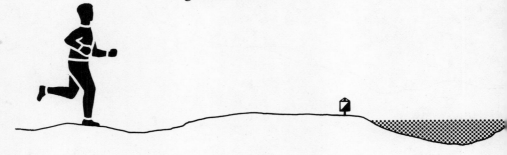

map
A map of the course is given to competitors before the race. Overprinted on the map, or printed on a separate sheet, are the locations of the controls, the out-of-bounds areas, and any other relevant information.
course
Orienteering courses vary considerably, but they are usually heavily-wooded areas; course lengths can range from 1–8 miles (1.60–12.87km). Details of the course are kept secret until the competition.

officials
Orienteering needs a large number of officials, the most important of whom is the course setter. In major events there is usually an official at each control point.
control points
The number of control points varies with the course. A control marker is usually a red and white flag (below). Each control is numbered.

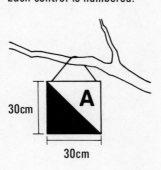

30cm

30cm

A

control card
Each competitor carries a control card which he stamps when he reaches a control.
compulsory tracks or paths
These are marked with tape or flags.
clothing
Track suits and studded running shoes are the most suitable clothes.

the start
Competitors assemble in a pre-start area and set off at intervals of 1–3 minutes.
duration
This varies with the type of competition. Some events end only when the course is completed; others have a time limit.

scoring
In point, relay, and line orienteering the competitor or team with the fastest time wins. Team scores are found by adding together the times of the team members. Score orienteering is performed in a strict time. In that time contestants visit as many controls as possible, each control having a points tariff varying from 5–50. Penalty points are deducted for every minute a competitor exceeds the time limit.

misconduct
Competitors are disqualified if they miss a control (except in score orienteering) or if they stamp their cards incorrectly.

compass
An orienteering compass should have the following characteristics.
1 Transparent base plate
2 Rotating compass housing
3 Orienteering lines
4 Direction marker
5 Magnifying lens
6 Distance·marker
7 Safety cord

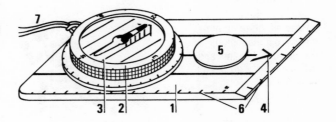

cross-country pointers

Cross-country running is strenuous, and like any event requires regular training. Above all you must keep yourself fit and well. Start any running session with a good warm-up and avoid getting cold afterward. Sleep is important, and so is diet. Avoid fatty, greasy foods before a race; often drinks and glucose are quite sufficient.

Endurance and determination are the keynotes to cross-country running; whether you are training or racing you should always complete the course.

Get to know the course before the race; check it out for hills, wet or dry ground, obstacles and possible bottlenecks. Pace judgement is vital, and tactics are much the same as for middle-distance running. Don't use up all your energy at the start of the race; work your way up through the runners to keep fairly close to the leaders. When you pass, do so in a determined fashion. Keep alert, and change your pace if you start to get tired. Use a short stride for uphill running, lengthening it to go downhill.

cross-country training

Training is mainly concerned with developing stamina and endurance; it consists largely of uphill running and walking, resistance running, and fartlek training.

You should try to run over as varied a terrain as possible (see below) so that you get used to running on different surfaces. You should also practice negotiating the types of obstacles that might occur during a race. As a general rule you should avoid leaping obstacles. Instead, hop down from embankments, run through streams and ditches, and vault over fences.

resistance running

This is for developing stamina, and entails running in heavy boots, or while wearing a weighted belt.

fartlek training

This is a type of interval running, and involves running over differing terrains at varying speeds. A typical session might include sprinting on a road, jogging through a wood, uphill running, and running over soft soil.

orienteering skills

For orienteering you need to be able to read a map and the topographical symbols on it, to relate the map to the ground it shows, and to navigate to any point on that map using distance and direction measurements. This obviously means that you need to know how to use an orienteering compass. The movable needle always swings to magnetic north, and the map is oriented by lining up the compass needle with the magnetic north lines marked on the map. Bearings can then be taken, and distances calculated from the scale given on the map. Your aim is to find the controls marked on the map and to visit them in the correct sequence. Often several routes will be possible, and you will have to decide, from the information given on the map, which is the best to use.

practice exercise

In orienteering every second counts. As a practice exercise you should get hold of an orienteering map and, using a compass, find out how long it takes to measure the distance and bearing of all the control points.

saving time

To save time you should know how long it takes you to cover a certain distance at varying speeds – sprinting, walking, striding or jogging. You can work this out yourself before an event, and attach the information to the top of your compass.

Sport for everyone

The enjoyment of athletics is by no means confined to able-bodied people. The thrill of competition and the wish to excell is present in every group of people, and this includes those who are handicapped in body or in mind. If you have lost the use of an arm you might have a little trouble with balance, but you are not prevented from running, hurdling, jumping etc.; if you have lost the use of a leg you can still take part in throwing events. The Stoke Mandeville Games for people confined to wheelchairs began with an archery contest in 1948, and they are now an annual event. Many different sports are included, and every four years the Games are linked as closely as possible to the Olympics.

paraplegics

Athletics events for the paralyzed at the Stoke Mandeville Games are the shot, discus, javelin, club throwing, 60m dash, 100m dash, 4 x 40m relay, and 4 x 60m relay. Women take part in all events except the 100m dash and the 4 x 60m relay. All the Olympic throwing events with the exception of the hammer are performed; instead of the hammer, a contest of club throwing has been devised. The club can be thrown from behind the shoulder, and does not have to be circled in the same way as a hammer.

blind athletes

Special race tracks can be set up to provide blind people with a safe, enjoyable way of competing effectively against one another by running. Instead of painted lane markings, the lanes are traced with tapes at about waist level; the athlete can feel the tape if he runs against it, and so can keep himself on course by touch.

Mentally handicapped people can be encouraged to participate in virtually all kinds of athletics at their own level. As well as improving their general health, athletics training also teaches them discipline, self-control and coordination, and an understanding of time and distance; in addition, the pride of achievement can be treasured by the mentally handicapped as much as by the skilled athlete. The Special Olympic Games are held every four years, and at them mentally handicapped adults and children can compete for medals. The ordinary Olympic track and field events are modified in the athletics section to fit the capabilities of the contestants; for instance, softball throwing takes the place of some of the more skilled throwing events.

Children of all ages thoroughly enjoy taking part in running and jumping games, and by doing so they will begin to develop the skills of speed, strength and timing that they can later channel into specific athletics events.

Use the enthusiasm of young children to the full to give them plenty of exercise, ideally in the open air; even the youngest ones will soon pick up the basic rules, and children catch on very quickly to the ideas of relays and team races. On the following pages we show you a selection of athletics-based games and sports for children that will help them to develop muscular co-ordination and the enjoyment of exertion.

Young children are easily bored, so avoid making the rules too complicated, and don't fuss about technical details such as style—if you do, the child's natural enjoyment will be inhibited and what should be a game will become a chore. Instead, aim to harness the child's natural vigor, so that he sees for himself the excitement of competition and the pleasure of activity—in this way he will grow into a healthy, active adolescent and a fit adult.

running games

Of course ordinary running races can be used for young children, but they will find them much more interesting if the race has some sort of novelty. The course could include a tree or post that the child has to run around, or the children can be divided into teams and a simple touch-relay organized. Three-legged races are also easy to organize.

Running games using objects are very popular with small children. Egg and spoon races and sack races can be run over short courses, and endless variety can be produced with obstacle races, when the children have to negotiate different objects. The obstacle course could include scrambling through tires or hoops, walking along a form, crawling under a sheet etc. — you will be able to devise many more challenges!

jumping games

Young children will not have the coordination for a formal type of high jump or long jump, but they will happily join in hopping, skipping or jumping races. A standing long jump can be organized by lining the children up and letting them jump as far as they can without a run-up. A kind of high jump can be played by giving each child in turn a piece of chalk and having him jump up and mark a wall or tree as high as he can—this is best played by children of roughly similar height.

throwing games

The basic game of "catch" has many variations. With very young children, use a fairly large, soft ball and let them throw and catch it with two hands; soon they will be able to graduate to just one.

Once children can throw and catch easily they can play piggy-in-the-middle, where one child tries to intercept the ball as it is thrown among the others. A target can be drawn on a tree or wall for the children to aim balls at; this will teach them accuracy and coordination. A softball can be used in contests of throwing for length.

If you want to practice athletics at home, or in a group such as a youth club, and you can't afford the standard equipment—don't despair! Equipment of all kinds can be improvised from everyday objects, and all your athletic skills can be practiced and improved using the makeshift jumps, weights, tracks etc.

The very important point to remember when you are using home-made equipment is that you must observe all the basic safety rules (see page 14) to ensure that you are not likely to injure yourself or others. In the following pages we give you various ideas for makeshift sports equipment. A few of the sports, such as pole vault and hammer throwing, are too dangerous to practice without professional supervision, but most other events can be improvised.

running
Temporary tracks can be laid out (on grass, ashphalt, or indoors) with string or twine. If you want to make a semipermanent track in a gymnasium the lines can be marked with paint or with white sticky tape; outdoors, longlasting tracks can be painted with creosote or white paint. Lanes, starting lines, staggered starts and relay zones can all be marked in the same way. Use a piece of tape held across the track at chest level for a finishing line.

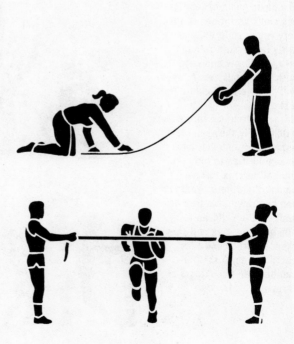

hurdles

Simple hurdles can be built from wood, but make sure that they will easily topple over if the runner touches them. For this reason they should only have horizontal balancing bars on the approach side, and the hurdle tops should be heavy so that they will topple easily.

jumping

High jumps can easily be simulated, but safety is important here as well. If a bar is used, it must only rest lightly on supports—not in holes—so that it will fall if the jumper knocks it even gently. If you are using a rope, either have it held by two people (who can let it go if the jumper touches it), or attach it to two light poles that are supported only on the outside; these will then fall gently inward if the rope is displaced. Make sure that you use plenty of foam mattresses for the landing area. Long jump and triple jump can be practiced using mattresses in place of sand.

throwing

For the shot put, the best substitute for a shot is a heavy stone; make sure that you can hold it comfortably so that it is not likely to slip. Use a straight bamboo or garden cane to practice the javelin grip and throw; bind the center to form a handgrip.

anchor-leg	Last leg of a relay.
baton	Hollow tube carried and passed on by relay runners.
bend	Curve in the running track.
calisthenics	Exercises for developing strength and mobility.
check marks	Indications placed by the track for judging run-ups etc.
control point	Marker that has to be visited on an orienteering course.
decathlon	Contest for men, comprising ten athletics events.
fartlek	Method of training involving untimed mixtures of sprinting, jogging and walking.
final	Ultimate round of any event.
glove	Protective grip used in hammer throwing.
heat	Preliminary round of any event.
IAAF	International Amateur Athletic Federation, the governing body of athletics.
interval running	Training method involving timed mixtures of sprinting, jogging and walking.
isometrics	Exercises involving static muscle tension.
lane	Subdivision of the running track allocated to each runner.

lap	One circuit of the track.
leg	Distance run by each competitor in a relay.
no jump	Disallowed trial in the jumping events.
pentathlon	Contest for women, comprising five athletics events.
plant	Placing of the pole when pole vaulting.
record	Best performance ever.
relay	Team race in which each competitor covers a portion of the total track.
resistance running	Training method involving running against a force such as a harness or weight.
scratch line	Marking line for field events and the start of track races.
staggered start	Method used when racing on a bend to ensure that all competitors run the same distance.
starting blocks	Foot blocks used by sprinters for fast starts.
takeover zone	Portion of the track within which the baton must be exchanged in a relay race.
wind assisted	Race run in a following wind over a certain velocity; no records may be claimed.